Access to
U.S. Government Information

Recent Titles in
Bibliographies and Indexes in Law and Political Science

Scottish Nationalism and Cultural Identity in the Twentieth Century:
An Annotated Bibliography of Secondary Sources
Gordon Bryan, compiler

Edward S. Corwin and the American Constitution: A Bibliographical Analysis
Kenneth D. Crews

Political Risk Assessment: An Annotated Bibliography
David A. Jodice, compiler

Human Rights: An International and Comparative Law Bibliography
Julian R. Friedman and Marc I. Sherman, compilers and editors

Latin American Society and Legal Culture
Frederick E. Snyder, compiler

Congressional Committees, 1789-1982: A Checklist
Walter Stubbs, compiler

Criminal Justice Documents: A Selective, Annotated Bibliography
of U.S. Government Publications Since 1975
John F. Berens, compiler

Terrorism, 1980-1987: A Selectively Annotated Bibliography
Edward F. Mickolus, compiler, with Peter A. Flemming

Guide to the *Archiv für Sozialwissenschaft und Sozialpolitik* Group, 1904-1933
Regis A. Factor

Contemporary Canadian Politics: An Annotated Bibliography, 1970-1987
Gregory Mahler, compiler

The Executive Branch of the U.S. Government: A Bibliography
Robert Goehlert and Hugh Reynolds, compilers

Access to
U.S. Government Information

Guide to Executive
and Legislative Authors and Authority

Compiled by
Jerrold Zwirn

Bibliographies and Indexes in Law and Political Science,
Number 12

Greenwood Press
Westport, Connecticut • London

Library of Congress Cataloging-in-Publication Data

Zwirn, Jerrold.
    Access to U.S. government information : guide to executive and
legislative authors and authority / compiled by Jerrold Zwirn.
        p. cm. — (Bibliographies and indexes in law and political
science, ISSN 0742-6909 ; no. 12)
        ISBN 0-313-26851-7 (lib. bdg. : alk. paper)
        1. Government publications—United States—Indexes. 2. United
States. Congress—Directories. 3. Administrative agencies—United
States—Directories. 4. Executive departments—United States—
Directories.   I. Title.   II. Series.
Z1223.Z7Z57   1989
[J83]
015.73' 053—dc20   89-27373

British Library Cataloguing in Publication Data is available.

Library of Congress Catalog Card Number: 89-27373
ISBN: 0-313-26851-7
ISSN: 0742-6909

First published in 1989

Greenwood Press, 88 Post Road West, Westport, CT 06881
An imprint of Greenwood Publishing Group, Inc.

Printed in the United States of America

∞™

The paper used in this book complies with the
Permanent Paper Standard issued by the National
Information Standards Organization (Z39.48-1984).

10 9 8 7 6 5 4 3 2

To Dee - for a difference I can see

Contents

Introduction

The federal government is the nation's foremost collector, classifier, producer, and distributor of information. Virtually all of it is available at little or no cost to those aware of its existence and issuer. However, the cost in time and effort can act as a deterrent. The multitude of governmental responsibilities and the magnitude of its organizational structure tend to impede, rather than expedite, public access to informational resources. A tool that pinpoints subjects, arrays authors, and correlates both can greatly simplify either the specific search or the general quest for desired data.

At one time or another everyone can profit from information available from an organizational unit of the federal government. Indeed, a prime reason for its distribution is to sustain public confidence in governmental performance and to enable recipients to personally benefit from its acquisition. However, the sheer mass of information generated, and the profusion of printed and automated tools aimed at its retrieval, may discourage an effort to obtain it. These factors may render the pursuit more laborious than might otherwise be the case. A convenient resource that can get the potential user off to a sure and smooth start is needed.

This volume endeavors to answer two questions: First, over which aspects of individual, organizational, national, and international affairs does the U.S. government exert authority or influence? Second, which units of the federal establishment are empowered to probe and pursue which matters? This guide aims to adequately cover and to maximize access to the realm of federal business. Its content and format offer a concise, yet complete, overview of contemporary public affairs and governmental policy agents.

Numerous publications contain information and advice on how and where to seek information from the federal government. Such handbooks and surveys are mainly arranged by subject category and issuing office. However useful these schemes are, both separately and in combination, they invariably involve some limitations in scope and depth. Although subject or office arrangement may encompass the full range of federal activity, the presentation of bibliographical data and office locations reduces the potential for inclusiveness and specificity. Consulting more than one source or resorting to multiple steps in the same source to determine which government authors are concerned with a given question is often necessary.

This guide provides comprehensive coverage of the topics and
affairs addressed by all key executive and legislative branch
units of the U.S. government. It identifies each entity that
exercises jurisdiction over a specific subject. The principal
purpose is to facilitate optimal access to the entire domain of
federal business and the corresponding sources of federal information. In addition this guide clarifies and classifies the
effects of concurrent and overlapping authority among governmental
offices. The approach is designed to record and reveal the relationship between formal powers and official authors.

Because the aims of this project differ from those pursued by
the U.S. Government Printing Office (GPO), it should be emphasized
that the definition of a government author also differs. The
primary factor used to determine a GPO author symbol is the agency
imprint or subunit autonomy. Author designation is linked to the
administrative status of its publications. In this guide the key
to authorship is the responsibility to formulate or implement
policy or to monitor or analyze conditions that pertain to a particular matter. Author identification is based on assigned duties.
An author is any federal unit whose mission or status obliges it to
create or collect information and to disclose or disseminate it.

The value of such a tool is determined by the selection of terms
to be used. The vast sphere and variety of governmental endeavor
would be a major obstacle if it were necessary to start from scratch.
However, this key task is expedited by the existence of four prominent indexes from which a nearly complete vocabulary can be compiled.
Each is prepared by a different government agency for a different
purpose. Their complementary nature enables the deficiencies of
each, however characterized, to be offset by the merits of the others.

One source is the GAO Thesaurus, issued in 1985. The General
Accounting Office is authorized to analyze and evaluate almost all
federal agencies as a means to improve functions and operations.
Its thesaurus is intended to aid public officials to retrieve
information about the performance of duties and units. Another
index is the Library of Congress subject headings in the Monthly
Catalog of U.S. Government Publications, issued annually by the
U.S. Government Printing Office. This entity is responsible for
the acquisition and distribution of most U.S. government information
products. Its Monthly Catalog is produced to assist private citizens
to locate material that can serve their needs.

Two other tabulations are subject indexes to the United States
·Code and the Code of Federal Regulations. The former is updated
every six years by the Office of the Law Revision Counsel, U.S.
House of Representatives, and the latter is revised annually by
the Office of the Federal Register, National Archives and Records
Administration. They provide access to existing laws and regulations,
respectively, that govern public and private rights and responsibilities. In contrast with the information and publication context of
the items described in the previous paragraph, these two are guides
to mandatory or permissible conduct. The legal requirements and
procedures covered by these tools offer another path from which to
approach federal jurisdiction and transactions.

Another major feature of this guide is its linkage of subjects
and authors. The following sources were consulted to ascertain
these relationships and to supplement the stock of entries derived
from the four indexes cited in the previous two paragraphs.

CIS/Index, published annually by Congressional Information
Service, Bethesda, MD.

Congressional Staff Directory, published semiannually by
Congressional Staff Directory, Ltd., Mount Vernon, VA.

Daily Digest, a separate volume of the bound Congressional
Record, published annually by the U.S. Government Printing Office.

Federal Information Sources and Systems, published by the U.S.
General Accounting Office in 1985.

Federal Staff Directory, published semiannually by Congressional
Staff Directory, Ltd., Mount Vernon, VA.

United States Government Manual, published annually by the Office
of the Federal Register, National Archives and Records Administration.

Washington Information Directory, published annually by Congressional Quarterly, Washington, DC.

Who Knows: A Guide to Washington Experts, published by Washington Researchers Publishing, Washington, DC, in 1986.

Although the above material furnished the basic data, decisions
were still necessary about whether to include or omit items and to
arrive at the preferred form of terms. This guide is noticeably
compact in comparison with the voluminous nature of those from
which it was compiled. Several reasons account for this size dif-
ferential. First, it is not geared for searching data bases or
pinpointing legal questions. Second, with few exceptions, proper
names, including agency titles, have been omitted. Third, there
are no see also references, which is explained further in the User
Guide that follows. While the devised subject listing may not
completely satisfy all who have an interest in the area of federal
information, the overall format offers several means of access and
can conveniently incorporate revisions.

In addition to the choice of entries, there was also the question
of how to determine whether the jurisdiction of a unit was suffi-
ciently extensive or important to be listed. A related question was
which offices should be listed when there existed concurrent authority between or among them. The answer to both entailed an intensive
examination of the sources cited in previous paragraphs with regard
to the clarity and frequency of their jurisdictional statements.
This still leaves some room for a degree of doubt in certain cases.
However, the overlap and consistency of these publications enables
one to assert with some confidence that the possibility of inaccura-
cies should not materially affect the guide's utility.

The major obstacle that confronts this or any other attempt to
organize and isolate discrete zones of federal endeavor is the
concept of program. Most governmental business and all funding is
tied to the unique nature of each program. Because it is a combination of purposes and processes it has thus far eluded efforts to
formulate a standard definition. In relation to programs, an entry
in this guide may include two or more, match the scope of an
existing one, or be unrelated to any.   For detailed information on
program authorization, administration, designation, and description,
one can consult the Budget of the U.S. Government - Appendix, issued
annually by the Office of Management and Budget, or the Catalog of
Federal Domestic Assistance, issued annually by the General Services
Administration.

Another factor that imposes limits on this type of undertaking
is the organic nature of government. Missions or titles may be
altered, reorganizations or mergers may be instituted, existing
entities may be abolished or new ones established. Even though
this ongoing process is dictated by the duty to meet emerging
public needs, its results are gradual and piecemeal. The effort
to balance organizational stability and adaptation ensures that
jurisdictional realignment generally preserves, rather than dis-
turbs, traditional administrative and political relationships.
That the inevitability of change is tempered by the advantages of
continuity prevents topical and organizational tabulations from
becoming quickly outdated. Each year the Senate Governmental
Affairs Committee issues a committee print on agencies and functions established, abolished, transferred or renamed by executive
or legislative action during the prior calendar year.

The schematic format of this work attempts to systematically depict existing relationships between public services and governmental sources. The use of a tandem subject and author approach enables users to quickly focus on functions assigned or implied by an official mandate. Its immediate goal is to assist those who plan to enter and explore the federal information thicket. Its ultimate goal is to devise a framework that can be adapted to the dynamic character of national governance and its information output.

This guide is intended to be used primarily for preliminary research purposes. However, when informational needs concern the concrete functions of a federal agency, another way exists to locate the appropriate office. The General Services Administration operates a nationwide network of federal information centers. These clearinghouses comprise a central source from which guidance may be obtained regarding all government services, programs, and regulations. When necessary to contact a federal office in reference to an immediate matter that is of a personal or professional nature, the nearest federal information center provides referrals to the government unit that offers relevant information or tangible assistance. A listing of all centers and their phone numbers appears in the United States Government Manual, a volume available at virtually every public library.

An additional way to obtain government information is through the Freedom of Information Act. It requires public officials to justify a decision to withhold information from those who submit a formal request. The act sets forth standards to determine which agency records must be released to the public and which can be kept confidential. It also provides administrative and judicial remedies when access is denied. This law applies only to agencies of the executive branch and not to elected officials or the federal judiciary. Those who seek material that has not been published or publicly distributed should consult A Citizen's Guide On Using The Freedom Of Information Act And The Privacy Act Of 1974 To Request Government Records, prepared by the House Government Operations Committee and issued as House Report 100-199, 100th Congress, 1st Session, 1987. It is available from the U.S. Government Printing Office.

To supplement information available from federal sources with that disseminated by nonfederal sources one may contact the National Referral Center (NRC). It is a free referral service for those who have specific questions on any topic. It maintains a subject-indexed database of some 15,000 organizations that possess specialized knowledge and are willing to provide information in their area of expertise. The NRC is not equipped to furnish substantive answers or to render bibliographic assistance. In response to requests submitted by mail, phone, or visit, a reply is usually transmitted within five working days. Its content includes a list of suggested offices to contact, including individual names and the type of information services offered. The address is: National Referral Center, Library of Congress, John Adams Building, Washington, DC 20540, (202) 707-5670.

User Guide

Subject access is the principal purpose of this guide. A key auxiliary goal is to chart the linkages among subjects, agencies, and committees. The following description and explanation covers three perspectives: 1) a review of the major features of each part, 2) an account of general factors that concern or pervade the entire project, and 3) a survey of those relationships that this guide is designed to illuminate.

Part 1 constitutes the core and bulk of this work, from which most of the other parts are derived. It is an alphabetical inventory of matters that command the attention or require the involvement of the U.S. government. The subject focus is neither subordinated to, nor restricted by, the inclusion of data readily available elsewhere. The result is a synoptic introduction to the roles and tasks assumed by the federal sector. See references are used as guides to broader or equivalent, but preferred, terms. Since these references are not repeated elsewhere, it is best to begin a subject search by perusing the left-hand column of entries and references. Where the precise meaning of a term is unclear, the numerical key that follows it, correlated with the general categories of Part 2, serves to clarify its usage by identifying its most salient dimension(s).

The order in which parent agencies are listed in Part 1/Column 2 is not entirely alphabetical. Cabinet departments appear first in alphabetical order, next is the Executive Office of the President when one of its subunits possesses authority, then all other agencies are entered in alphabetical sequence. This arrangement generally gives a more accurate picture of agency predominance in descending order than would a strictly alphabetical scheme. Nonetheless, this structural relationship does not apply in all cases.

Part 2 groups the specific entries of Part 1 under 20 general subject headings. This grouping represents an effort to produce a refined list of subject categories unaffected by the historical and political factors that shape agency and committee jurisdiction and is intended to aid those whose information needs cover a wide range of related activities, multiple aspects, and mutual effects. Another aim is to eliminate the need for see also references in Part 1, since related terms are clustered for a more convenient overview of a broad policy sphere. The interdependent nature of, and shared assignment over, many responsibilities means that numerous terms appear under more than one general subject heading.

Consult Part 1, however, to identify entities having authority over each entry in Part 2.

Since the terms in Part 1 do not include all possible variations under which a given subject may be entered, the following expedient may be helpful when a certain term is not listed. First, determine which of the general subject categories of Part 2 is most likely to cover the specific topic that is being researched. Then scan the entries under that heading in Section 1 to ascertain which most closely matches the meaning of the one at hand.

Parts 3 and 4 are aimed at those for whom an administrative agency or congressional committee approach is convenient or neces- sary. The second section of Parts 2-5 each chart some associated relationships that merit attention in the context of federal inter- action and information. They correlate authors to fill potential gaps that can stem from a straight subject survey. Although this might result in some repetition, on the whole it contributes to easier retrieval of and simplified searching for desired data.

Part 5 affirms that Appropriations Committee hearings are a major source of information on all aspects of public activity. In a technical sense the appropriations panels do not exercise authority over substantive policy since their jurisdiction is based on agency budgets rather than subject areas. However, the focus on past and proposed spending necessarily entails an exami- nation of program management and output which yields an information product that supplements more topically oriented ones.

The entries in Part 1/Column 6 do not cite all appropriations subcommittees that would seem to be warranted by Part 5/Section 2. In only six cases are more than two panels listed. This is because those having jurisdiction over agencies with comparatively modest or stable expenditures are unlikely to generate information that is substantive, rather than administrative, in nature. The appropri- ations subcommittee structure is identical in each house of Congress.

In addition to its normal use, the Index serves some additional purposes. Some agency subunits exercise authority over more sub- ject areas than some parent agencies. These major subunits can be identified by noting the page number references to Part 1. The Index can also be used to compile a list of subunits for major parent agencies; to match agency subunits with congressional com- mittees when more than one panel exercises jurisdiction over a single agency; and to facilitate the isolation, combination, or comparison of certain entities to meet particular research needs.

An important feature of federal jurisdiction is the partition of authority between or among offices based on some traditional or natural divisions of many subject categories. Those pairs of con- cepts that most commonly bisect a domain or function are its public/private, domestic/international, civil/military, financial/ substantive, regulatory/research, or policy/agency components. In the large majority of cases which offices exercise jurisdiction over which components is usually clear.

Where the distinction between components is not evident, the citation of certain committees provides a key clue. For the first dichotomy, the House Government Operations and Senate Governmental Affairs committees indicate a public element; for the second, the House Foreign Affairs and Senate Foreign Relations committees indicate an international one; for the third, the Armed Services committees indicate a military one; for the fourth, the House Ways and Means and Senate Finance committees indicate a financial one. For the fifth, to recognize those agencies that are primarily research units is necessary. These entities include the four congressional support agencies (Congressional Budget Office, General Accounting Office, Library of Congress, and Office of Technology Assessment); three subunits of the Executive Office of the President (Council of Economic Advisers, Council on

Environmental Quality, and Science and Technology Policy Office);
two independent entities (National Science Foundation and Smith-
sonian Institution); and a subunit of the Commerce Department
(National Institute of Standards and Technology). The last
dichotomy is most clearly reflected in the division of responsibility between the Appropriations panels and all other committees,
while the House Government Operations and Senate Governmental
Affairs committees may examine a matter from either perspective.

There are several committees and agencies whose jurisdiction
encompasses nearly the entire spectrum of federal activities.
Nonetheless in this guide they are listed only under those subject areas in which they play a prominent role. That they may
issue valuable information relating to matters that are not
readily associated with their title is a fact that should not
be overlooked. These units include the Appropriations and Budget
committees in both houses of Congress, the House Government Operations and Ways and Means committees, the Senate Finance and Governmental Affairs committees, the Congressional Budget Office, and the
General Accounting Office.

Some offices have only a secondary interest in some subjects
or activities. This occurs when minor responsibilities consume
a small proportion of the unit's resources. In such instances
its level of participation is limited to providing support for,
or coordinating operations with, those entities for which it is
a primary concern. Where its status is subsidiary or subordinate,
the extent of its role does not warrant its inclusion in this
survey since the information it generates or releases will be
available in more complete form from the office(s) that deal
with the matter directly and continually.

All agencies have a public affairs office, many of which issue
periodicals or general publications that cover organizational
business. In many agencies information originates in operational
units, but is distributed through a central organ. This guide
does not list staff offices that coordinate the information
resources or arrangements of particular authors. The focus is
on substantive responsibility, with informational structure taken
into account only when it is an integral part of prescribed functions. For similar reasons those offices responsible for internal
matters such as administrative efficiency, budgeting, personnel,
and legal questions are also omitted.

Temporary and advisory bodies are excluded from this guide.
This is not because they do not issue useful information. The
brief existence and eventual expiration of interim units outweigh
their role as government authors in a list of permanent offices.
Most of the information that originates with advisory units is
channeled through the offices with which they are formally con-
nected. The column of agency subunits in Part 1 cites those that
are closest to the subject entry, which means that titles of
administrative units in the hierarchy between a parent agency and
a given subdivision are omitted. Congressional subcommittees,
except for the appropriations panels, are not listed because of
their susceptibility to reorganization or redesignation, and
because citations to legislative information are normally to
the full committee.

Another type of unit created by Congress to meet public needs
is omitted from this guide. These entities, though sponsored by
a government agency, are privately owned and mainly privately
funded. Their legal and financial status excludes them from
membership in the family of federal authors. Among the more
prominent of these bodies are the Federal National Mortgage
Association and Neighborhood Reinvestment Corporation, both
monitored by the Housing and Urban Development Department; the
Public Broadcasting Corporation and Student Loan Marketing Association, both monitored by the Education Department; the National
Railroad Passenger Corporation (AMTRAK), monitored by the

Transportation Department; and the Securities Investor Protection
Corporation, monitored by the Securities and Exchange Commission.

Other than the opinions issued by specific courts, there are
basically three authors that comprise the federal judiciary. One
is the Judicial Conference of the United States, the policymaking
arm of the judiciary, chaired by the Chief Justice of the United
States. Another, the Administrative Office of the United States
Courts, is responsible for monitoring and managing judicial administration and preparing reports on workload, resources, practices,
and results. One other is the Federal Judicial Center, created to
meet the research and educational needs of the judiciary. Although
not otherwise cited in this guide, their publications cover all
aspects of the national court system and the matters under its
jurisdiction. The large majority of those subjects addressed by
judicial authors appears in Part 2/Section 1 under the heading of
Legal Affairs.

The relationships that form the body of this guide are listed
below. Each pair of terms is followed by a statement about how to
link them, starting with the item on the left. A tabular summary
of uses presents an overview of information purposes served and of
research options addressed.

Specific Subject -
    General Subject: Part 1/Column 1, then match numerical codes
                      with codes in Part 2/Section 1.
    Parent Agency: Part 1/Column 2.
    Legislative Committee: Part 1/Columns 4 & 5.
    Appropriations Subcommittee: Part 1/Column 6.

General Subject -
    Specific Subject: Part 2/Section 1.
    Parent Agency: Part 2/Section 2/Column 2.
    Legislative Committee: Part 2/Section 2/Columns 3 & 4.
    Appropriations Subcommittee: Part 2/Section 2/Column 5.

Parent Agency -
    Specific Subject: Part 3/Section 1.
    General Subject: Part 3/Section 2, then match numerical codes
                      with codes in Part 2/Section 1 or 2.
    Legislative Committee: Part 3/Section 2/Columns 2 & 3.
    Appropriations Subcommittee: Part 3/Section 2/Column 4.

Legislative Committee -
    Specific Subject: Part 4/Section 1.
    General Subject: Part 4/Section 2, then match numerical codes
                      with codes in Part 2/Section 1 or 2.
    Parent Agency: Part 4/Section 2/Column 2.
    Appropriations Subcommittee: Part 4/Section 2/Column 4.

Appropriations Subcommittee -
    Specific Subject: Part 5/Section 1.
    General Subject: Part 5/Section 2, then match numerical codes
                      with codes in Part 2/Section 1 or 2.
    Parent Agency: Part 5/Section 2/Column 2.
    Legislative Committee: Part 5/Section 2/Columns 3 & 4.

The absence of a subject index is compensated for by two features.
One is the alphabetical listing of specific subject categories in
Part 1. The other is the listing of numerical codes combined with
the entries under columns 2, 4, 5, and 6 of Part 1. This data serves
as a guide to the same specific subject categories in Section 1 of
Parts 2-5.

Access to
U.S. Government Information

Part 1

**Executive and Legislative Jurisdiction
by Specific Subject Category**

	Parent Agencies	Agency Subunits	House Committees	Senate Committees	Appropriations Subcommittees
Abortion (11, 14)	HHS	PHS	JU	JU	LAB
Abuse of authority. See Inspectors General					
Accidents. See Aviation safety, Highway safety, Marine safety, Occupational safety, Product safety, Railroad safety					
Accounting (9, 10)	TRE TRE EOP GAO SEC	FMS IRS OMB	EN, GO, WM	BA, FI, GA	COM, TRE
Accreditation. See Higher education					
Acid rain (8, 16)	EOP EPA	CEQ	EN	EP	VA
Acquired immune deficiency syndrome (AIDS) (11)	HHS HHS HHS HHS	CDC FDA MCHRD NIAI	EN	LA	LAB
Addiction. See Alcoholism, Drug abuse, Smoking					
Additives. See Food inspection					
Administrative law (10, 14)	ACUS		GO, JU	GA, JU	TRE
Administrative management. See Public administration					
Admiralty law. See Maritime industry					
Adoption. See Family services					
Adult education (5)	EDU EDU	PE VAE	ED	LA	LAB
Adulteration. See Food inspection					
Advertising (2, 3)	HHS TRE FCC FTC SEC	FDA ATF	BA, EN	BA, CO	COM
Advisory committees (10)	GSA	CMS	GO	GA	TRE
Aeronautics (17, 19)	EOP NASA SI	STP	SC	CO	VA
Affirmative action. See Civil rights					
Aged (12, 18)	HHS HHS HHS	AA NIA SSA	AGI, ED, EN, WM	AGI, FI, LA	LAB

	Parent Agencies	Agency Subunits	House Committees	Senate Committees	Appropriations Subcommittees
Agricultural credit (1, 9, 12)	AGR AGR FCA	FAHA REA	AG	AG	AGR
Agricultural development (1, 4)	AGR AGR	ACS ES	AG	AG	AGR
Agricultural markets (1, 13)	AGR AGR	AMS FAS	AG	AG	AGR
Agricultural production (1)	AGR AGR	AMS ASCS	AG	AG	AGR
Agricultural research (1, 17)	AGR AGR	ARS NAL	AG, SC	AG	AGR
Agricultural subsidies (1, 12)	AGR AGR	ASCS CCC	AG	AG	AGR
Agricultural surpluses (1, 13, 18)	AGR AGR AGR	CCC FAS FNS	AG	AG	AGR
Air Force. See Armed forces					
Air pollution (8, 11, 16, 17)	COM TRA EPA	NOAA FAA	EN, SC	EP	COM, VA
Aircraft. See Aviation safety					
Airlines. See Aviation industry					
Airports (4, 19)	TRA	FAA	PW	CO	TRA
Airspace (13, 15)	DEF STA STA	AF LAO PMA	AR, FA	AR, FR	COM
Alcoholic beverages (2, 14)	TRE	ATF	EN, JU	CO, JU	TRE
Alcoholism (11)	HHS	NIAA	EN	LA	LAB
Aliens (6, 14)	JUS LAB	INS ILA	ED, JU	JU, LA	COM, LAB
Allergies (11)	HHS	NIAI	EN	LA	LAB
Alliances. See Treaties					
American history. See Federal records, Historic preservation, Museums					
Animals (11, 16)	AGR HHS INT SI	APHIS FDA FWS	AG, MM	AG, EP	AGR, INT
Annuities. See Pensions					
Antibiotics. See Drug safety					

	Parent Agencies	Agency Subunits	House Committees	Senate Committees	Appropriations Subcommittees
Antitrust law (2, 14)	JUS FCC FTC ICC	ANT	EN, JU, SB	CO, JU, SB	COM
Apparel industry. See Product labeling					
Appellate courts. See Federal courts					
Appliances. See Energy conservation					
Apprenticeship (6)	LAB EEOC	ETA	ED	LA	LAB
Arbitration. See Labor relations					
Archeological sites. See Historic preservation					
Architecture (5, 10)	INT FAC GSA NFAH	NPS PBS	ED, GO	GA, LA	INT
Archives. See Federal records					
Armament. See Weapons					
Armed forces (15)	DEF DEF DEF	AF ARMY NAVY	AR	AR	DEF
Arms control (13, 15)	DEF ENER STA EOP ACDA	NFAC DPO PMA NSC	AR, FA	AR, FR	COM, DEF
Arms exports (13, 15)	DEF DEF STA STA ACDA	DLA ISA EBA PMA	AR, FA	AR, FR	DEF, FA
Army. See Armed forces					
Arson (14)	TRE FEMA	ATF	JU	GA, JU	TRE, VA
Arthritis (11)	HHS	NIAM	EN	LA	LAB
Artificial intelligence. See Computer technology					
Arts (3, 5)	NFAH SI		ED, HA	LA, RU	INT
Asbestos (6, 11)	LAB EPA	OSHA	ED, EN	EP, LA	LAB, VA
Astronautics. See Aeronautics					

	Parent Agencies	Agency Subunits	House Committees	Senate Committees	Appropriations Subcommittees
Astronomy (17)	DEF NASA NSF	NAVO	SC	CO	VA
Athletics. See Sports					
Atmosphere (8, 17)	COM TRA EPA NASA NSF	NOAA FAA	EN, SC	CO, EP	COM, VA
Atomic energy. See Nuclear energy					
Audio equipment. See Recording industry					
Auditing. See Accounting					
Authors. See Copyrights					
Automation. See Industrial technology					
Automobile industry (2, 11, 19)	TRA EPA FTC	NHTSA	EN, PW	CO, EP	COM, TRA
Aviation industry (2, 19)	TRA	FAA	EN, PW, SC	CO, EP	TRA
Aviation safety (11, 17)	TRA NTSB	FAA	PW	CO	TRA
Bacteriology (11)	HHS	NIAI	EN	LA	LAB
Balance of payments. See International trade					
Bank deposits (9)	FDIC FSLIC		BA	BA	VA
Bank notes. See Currency					
Bank regulation (9)	TRE FHLBB FRB	CC	BA	BA	TRE, VA
Bank reserves. See Money supply					
Bankruptcy (9, 14)	JUS JUS SEC	CID LIA	JU	JU	COM
Beaches. See Recreation areas					
Bicycles. See Product safety					
Bilingual education (5)	EDU	BE	ED	LA	LAB
Bill of Rights. See Capital punishment, Eminent domain, Juries, Law enforcement, Privacy, Trials					
Billboards (2, 3)	TRA	FEHA	PW	EP	TRA

	Parent Agencies	Agency Subunits	House Committees	Senate Committees	Appropriations Subcommittees
Biotechnology (17)	COM HHS HHS EOP NSF OTA	NIST FDA NIGM STP	SC	CO, LA	COM, LAB
Birds (16)	AGR INT	APHIS FWS	AG, IN	AG, EP	AGR, INT
Birth control. See Abortion, Family planning, Population growth					
Birth defects. See Prenatal care					
Black market. See Commercial law					
Blindness. See Disability benefits, Handicapped, Visual disorders					
Blood (11)	HHS HHS	FDA NHL	EN	LA	LAB
Boating. See Marine safety					
Bonds. See Government securities, Public debt, Securities industry					
Books. See Copyrights					
Border patrol (13, 14)	JUS TRE	INS CS	FA, JU	FR, JU	COM, TRE
Borrowing. See Consumer credit, Government borrowing, Securities industry					
Brain disorders. See Handi- capped, Mental health, Neurological diseases					
Brand names. See Trademarks					
Bridges (4, 19)	TRA TRA TRA	CG FEHA FRA	PW	EP	TRA
Broadcasting (2, 3)	COM FCC	NTIA	EN	CO	COM
Brokerage firms. See Securities industry					
Budget administration (9, 10)	TRE EOP GAO	FMS OMB	AP, GO, WM	AP, FI, GA	TRE
Budget deficits (9, 10)	TRE EOP CBO	PDB OMB	BU, WM	BU, FI	TRE

	Parent Agencies	Agency Subunits	House Committees	Senate Committees	Appropriations Subcommittees
Budget formulation (9, 10)	TRE EOP EOP CBO	EPO CEA OMB	BU, GO, RU	BU, GA	TRE
Building standards (11, 17, 20)	COM HUD	NIST MHS	BA	BA	COM, VA
Bus lines (2, 19)	ICC		EN	CO	TRA
Business assistance (2, 4)	COM TRA TRA EXIM FEMA SBA	EDA FRA MA	BA, PW, SB	BA, EP, SB	COM, TRA
Business ethics. See Consumer protection					
Business failures. See Bankruptcy					
Business income. See Taxation					
Business investment (9)	COM TRE SBA SEC	EAB IRS	BA, EN, SB, WM	BA, CO, FI, SB	COM, TRE
Business regulation (2)	FCC FTC ICC SBA		EN, SB	CO, SB (JEC)	COM
Cable television. See Broadcasting					
Campaign finance. See Elections					
Campgrounds. See Recreation areas					
Canals. See Inland waterways					
Cancer (11)	HHS	NCI	EN	LA	LAB
Capital formation. See Business investment					
Capital gains. See Taxation					
Capital punishment (14)	JUS	LIA	JU	JU	COM
Capitol facilities (10)	ARC		HA, PW	EP, RU	LEG
Cardiology. See Heart disease					
Career counseling. See Vocational education					
Cargo. See Freight					
Cartography. See Mapping					
Censorship. See Government information					

	Parent Agencies	Agency Subunits	House Committees	Senate Committees	Appropriations Subcommittees
Census (10)	COM	CB	PO	GA	COM
Charitable organizations (3, 18)	TRE PS	IRS	PO, WM	FI, GA	TRE
Checking accounts. See Money supply					
Checks. See Negotiable instruments					
Chemicals (11, 17)	COM LAB EPA NSF OTA	NIST OSHA	ED, EN, SC	CO, LA	COM, VA
Child abuse (18)	HHS	CYFA	ED	LA	LAB
Child care. See Day care					
Child custody. See Family services					
Child health (11, 18)	HHS HHS HHS	DDA MCHRD NICH	EN	LA	LAB
Child nutrition (18)	AGR	FNS	AG, ED	AG	AGR
Child support (12, 18)	HHS	FSA	ED	LA	LAB
Cities. See Local governments					
Citizens abroad (13)	STA	CAB	FA	FR	COM
Citizens band radio. See Telecommunications					
Citizenship (10, 14)	JUS STA	INS CAB	JU	JU	COM
Civil defense (15)	DEF TRA FEMA	DCPA CG	AR	AR	DEF, VA
Civil disorders (14)	JUS JUS FEMA	FBI MS	JU	JU	COM
Civil procedure (14)	JUS	LIA	JU	JU	COM
Civil rights (14)	JUS CRC	CRD	JU	JU	COM
Civil Service. See Government employees					
Civil-military relations (10)	EOP LC	NSC CRS	FA, JU	FR, JU	TRE
Class action. See Consumer protection					
Classified information. See Government information					

	Parent Agencies	Agency Subunits	House Committees	Senate Committees	Appropriations Subcommittees
Climate. See Atmosphere, Environmental research, Weather					
Coal (7, 8, 16)	ENER ENER INT INT INT INT	ERA FEO GS LMB MMS SMRE	EN, IN, SC	EN, EP	ENER, INT
Coastal zone management (16, 17)	COM DEF	NOAA ACE	IN, MM	CO, EN	COM
Cocaine. See Drug abuse, Drug testing, Drug traffic					
Coinage. See Currency					
Coins. See Numismatics					
Collective bargaining. See Labor relations					
Colleges. See Higher education					
Commercial banks. See Financial institutions					
Commercial law (2, 14)	JUS FTC ICC	CID	BA, EN, JU, SB (JEC)	BA, CO, JU, SB	COM
Commercial paper. See Negotiable instruments					
Commodity regulation (1, 2)	CFTC		AG	AG	AGR
Communicable diseases (11)	HHS HHS HHS	CDC NIAI HRSA	EN	LA	LAB
Compensation. See Fringe benefits, Pensions, Wages					
Compensatory education (5)	EDU EDU	CEP PE	ED	LA	LAB
Computer security (14, 17)	COM JUS EOP GSA	NIST ITO OMB IRMS	GO, JU, SC	GA, JU,	COM, TRE
Computer technology (3, 17)	COM EOP GPO GSA NSF OTA	NIST STP IRMS	GO, SC	CO, GA	COM, VA
Condominiums. See Housing management					
Conflicts of interest. See Government ethics					
Conglomerates. See Commercial law					

	Parent Agencies	Agency Subunits	House Committees	Senate Committees	Appropriations Subcommittees
Congressional districts (10)	COM	CB	JU	JU	COM
Congressional employees (6, 10)	JUS JUS	CID CRID	HA	RU	LEG
Congressional ethics. See Members of Congress					
Congressional operations (10)	GAO LC	CRS	GO, HA, RU	GA, RU	LEG
Congressional organization (10)	LC	CRS	GO, RU	GA, RU	LEG
Congressional oversight (10)	GAO LC	CRS	GO, RU	GA, RU	LEG
Congressional power (10, 14)	JUS LC	AG CRS	JU	JU	LEG
Congressional-executive relations (10, 14)	JUS EOP GAO LC	AG OMB CRS	FA, GO, JU, RU	FR, GA, JU, RU	LEG, TRE
Conscientious objectors. See Selective Service					
Conservation. See Energy conservation, Environmental protection, Land management, Soil conservation, Wilderness areas, Wildlife conservation					
Constitutional amendments (14)	JUS	AG	JU	JU	COM, LEG
Construction industry (11, 20)	HUD HUD LAB	UDAG URO OSHA	BA, ED	BA, LA	VA
Consumer credit (9, 14)	TRE FDIC FHLBB FRB FTC NCUA	CC	BA, EN	BA, CO	COM
Consumer education (5)	AGR HHS CPSC FTC GSA	ARS FDA CIC	AG, EN, GO	AG, CO, GA	COM, VA
Consumer Price Index (9)	LAB	LSB	ED (JEC)	LA	LAB
Consumer protection (2, 11)	CPSC FTC		EN	CO	COM, VA
Contraband. See Smuggling					
Contracts. See Government contracts, Inspectors General, Public administration					
Cooperative housing. See Housing management					

	Parent Agencies	Agency Subunits	House Committees	Senate Committees	Appropriations Subcommittees
Copyrights (3, 14)	STA CRT LC	EBA COPY	JU	JU	COM, LEG
Corporate assets. See Taxation					
Corporate debt. See Securities industry					
Corporate mergers. See Commercial law					
Correctional facilities (14)	JUS JUS JUS	JAB NIC PB	JU	JU	COM
Corrupt practices (10, 14)	JUS JUS JUS	CRID EOUS FBI	HA, JU, ST	ET, JU	COM, LEG
Cosmetics industry (11)	HHS	FDA	EN	CO, LA	AGR
Cotton. See Fibers					
Counterfeiting (14)	TRE TRE	EPB SS	JU	JU	TRE
Counties. See Local governments					
Courts. See Federal courts					
Covert action. See Intelligence activities					
Credit bureaus. See Consumer protection					
Credit cards. See Consumer credit					
Credit programs (4, 9, 20)	TRE EOP CBO GAO	FMS OMB	AP, BA, BU	AP, BA, BU	TRE
Credit unions (9)	FRB NCUA		BA	BA	VA
Crime data (14)	JUS JUS	FBI JSB	JU	JU	COM
Crime prevention (5)	JUS JUS	JAB NIJ	JU	JU	COM
Crime victims (12, 14)	JUS JUS FEMA	JAB JPO	BA, JU	BA, JU	COM
Criminal investigations. See Law enforcement					
Criminal procedure (14)	JUS	LIA	JU	JU	COM
Crops (1, 12)	AGR AGR	ARS FCIC	AG	AG	AGR

	Parent Agencies	Agency Subunits	House Committees	Senate Committees	Appropriations Subcommittees
Demography. See Census					
Dentistry (11)	HHS	NID	EN	LA	LAB
Deportation (14)	JUS	INS	JU	JU	COM
Deposit insurance. See Bank deposits					
Depository institutions. See Financial institutions					
Depreciation. See Taxation					
Depressed areas (4, 20)	COM HUD HUD	EDA BGA PDR	BA, PW	BA, EP	COM, VA
Devaluation. See International finance					
Developing countries. See Foreign aid					
Diamonds. See Precious stones					
Diet. See Nutrition					
Diplomatic immunity (13, 14)	JUS STA	LIA PO	FA, JU	FR, JU	COM
Diplomatic recognition (13)	STA STA	PMA PO	FA	FR	COM
Diplomatic service (10, 13)	STA STA	FMO FSE	FA	FR	COM
Disability benefits (12, 18)	HHS VA	SSA VBA	ED, VA	LA, VA	LAB, VA
Disabled. See Handicapped					
Disarmament. See Arms control					
Disaster relief (4, 12, 13)	AGR FEMA IDCA SBA	FAHA AID	AG, FA, PW, SB	AG, EP, FR, SB	AGR, VA
Discrimination (14)	EDU HHS HUD LAB EEOC	CRO CRO FHEO CRO	BA, ED, EN, JU	BA, CO, JU, LA	COM, LAB
Disease control. See Communicable diseases					
District of Columbia (10, 20)	NCPC PADC		AP, DC, IN, PW	AP, EP, GA	DC
Divestiture. See Commercial law					
Dividends. See Taxation					
Draft. See Selective Service					

	Parent Agencies	Agency Subunits	House Committees	Senate Committees	Appropriations Subcommittees
Drinking water. See Water supply					
Drought. See Crops					
Drug abuse (11, 18)	HHS	NIDA	EN	LA	LAB
Drug safety (11, 17)	HHS OTA	FDA	EN	LA	AGR
Drug testing (6, 11, 17)	DEF HHS LAB EOP OPM OTA	HAO NIDA LMR STP	AR, EN, GO, PO	AR, CO, GA, LA	LAB, TRE
Drug traffic (13, 14)	DEF JUS JUS JUS JUS JUS JUS STA TRA TRE EOP	CCCI CRID DEA FBI INS INTER JAB INM CG CS NDC	FA, JU	FR, JU	COM, TRE
Drunk driving. See Highway safety					
Earth sciences. See Atmosphere, Geology, Oceanography					
Earthquake damage. See Disaster relief					
Earthquake research (8, 17)	INT NSF	GS	IN, SC	CO, EP	INT
Eating disorders (11)	HHS	NIDD	EN	LA	LAB
Ecology. See Environmental protection					
Economic controls (2, 9)	TRE EOP	EPO CEA	BA	BA	TRE
Economic data (1, 2, 6, 9)	AGR AGR COM COM COM LAB EOP CBO FRB SBA SEC	ERS NASS CB EAB IEB LSB CEA	AG, BA, BU, ED (JEC)	AG, BA, BU, LA	AGR, COM, LAB
Economic risk. See Business assistance, Credit programs, Insurance programs					
Economic sanctions. See International trade					

	Parent Agencies	Agency Subunits	House Committees	Senate Committees	Appropriations Subcommittees
Education data (5)	EDU	NCES	ED	LA	LAB
Education research (5)	EDU EDU	ERI NIE	ED	LA	LAB
Elderly. See Aged					
Elections (10)	JUS FEC	CRID	HA, JU	JU, RU	LEG, TRE
Electric power (7, 17)	ENER TVA	FERC	EN, IN, PW, SC	EN, EP	ENER
Electrical standards (17)	COM NSF	NIST	SC	CO	COM, VA
Electronic data processing. See Computer technology					
Electronic fund transfers. See Financial institutions					
Electronic surveillance. See Privacy					
Elementary education (5)	EDU	ESE	ED	LA	LAB
Embargoes. See International trade					
Embassies. See Diplomatic service					
Emergency preparedness. See Civil defense					
Eminent domain (10, 14)	JUS TRE	LNR IRS	GO, PW	EP, GA	COM
Employee benefits. See Fringe benefits					
Employer liability. See Workers compensation					
Employment data. See Economic data					
Endangered species (16)	AGR COM INT	FS NOAA FWS	IN, MM, SC	CO, EP	COM, INT
Energy conservation (7, 17)	COM ENER HUD	NIST CRE EEO	EN	EN	ENER
Energy consumption (2, 7)	ENER ENER	ERA FERC	EN	EN	ENER, INT
Energy data (7)	ENER	EIA	EN	EN	INT
Energy prices (2, 7)	ENER ENER	ERA FERC	EN	EN	ENER, INT
Energy production (2, 7, 17)	ENER INT EOP OTA	FERC MMS STP	EN, IN	EN	ENER, INT

	Parent Agencies	Agency Subunits	House Committees	Senate Committees	Appropriations Subcommittees
Energy research (7, 17)	ENER INT EOP NSF OTA	ERO GS STP	EN, SC	EN	ENER, INT
Energy reserves. See Resource shortages					
Energy storage (7, 8)	ENER EPA	ESH	EN	EN	ENER, VA

Engineering. See Computer
  technology, Industrial
  technology, Technology
  transfer					

Environmental protection (8, 11)	AGR COM INT JUS EPA	FS NOAA FWS LNR	EN, IN	EN, EP	INT, VA
Environmental research (8, 17)	COM ENER HHS HUD STA EOP EPA NSF OTA	NOAA ESH NIEH EEO OIE CEQ	IN, MM, SC	CO, EP	COM, VA
Epidemiology (11)	HHS	CDC	EN	LA	LAB
Espionage (13, 14)	JUS JUS EOP	CRID FBI CIA	FA, JU	FR, JU	COM, DEF
Estates and trusts. See Taxation					
Estuaries. See Coastal zone management					
Exchange rates. See Foreign currency					
Excises. See Taxation					
Executive agreements. See International agreements					
Executive branch operations (10)	EOP GAO GSA	OMB	AP, GO	AP, GA	TRE
Executive branch organization (10)	EOP	OMB	GO	GA	TRE
Executive power. See Presidency					
Executive privilege (10, 14)	JUS EOP	AG WHO	GO, JU	GA, JU	COM, TRE
Expatriation (14)	JUS STA	CID CAB	FA, JU	FR, JU	COM

	Parent Agencies	Agency Subunits	House Committees	Senate Committees	Appropriations Subcommittees
Expenditures. See Government spending					
Explosives (11, 14, 17)	LAB TRE CPSC	MSHA ATF	ED, JU, SC	CO, JU,	COM, TRE
Exports (2, 13)	AGR COM DEF ENER STA EOP EXIM ITC	FAS EXP DTSA DPO EBA TRO	AG, BA, EN, FA, SB	AG, BA, CO, FR, SB	COM, FA
Expositions (2, 13)	COM USIA	ITA	EN, FA	CO, FR	COM
Extortion. See Organized crime					
Extradition (13, 14)	JUS JUS STA	CRID INTER LEI	FA, JU	FR, JU	COM
Factories. See Occupational safety					
Family farms. See Agricultural credit					
Family planning (18)	HHS HHS	HRSA PHS	EN	LA	LAB
Family services (18)	HHS HHS HHS	FSA FYS SSA	ED	LA	LAB
Farm labor. See Migrant workers					
Farming. See Agricultural development					
Federal charters (14)	JUS	CID	JU	JU	COM
Federal courts (10, 14)	JUS	LIA	JU	JU	COM
Federal judges (10, 14)	JUS	AG	JU	JU	COM
Federal paperwork (10)	TRE EOP	IRS OMB	GO, PO, WM	FI, GA	TRE
Federal property (10)	GSA GSA	FPR FSS	GO	GA	TRE
Federal records (3, 10)	LC NARA		GO, HA	GA, RU	TRE
Federalism. See Intergovernmental relations					
Ferries. See Water transportation					
Fibers (1)	AGR AGR	AMS ASCS	AG	AG	AGR

	Parent Agencies	Agency Subunits	House Committees	Senate Committees	Appropriations Subcommittees
Financial institutions (9)	TRE TRE FDIC FHLBB FRB FSLIC NCUA SEC	CC DFO	BA	BA	TRE, VA
Financial management. See Budget administration					
Financial markets. See Securities industry					
Fire control (16, 17)	AGR COM FEMA	FS NIST	AG, SC	AG, CO	COM, INT
Fire damage. See Disaster relief					
Firearms (14)	TRE	ATF	JU	JU	COM, TRE

Fiscal policy. See Debt
  management, Government
  spending, Taxation					

Fish. See Wildlife conservation					
Fishing. See Maritime industry					
Flag of the U.S. (10)	EOP	WHO	JU	JU	TRE
Flammable materials. See Product safety					
Flood control (8, 16)	AGR COM DEF INT TVA	SCS NOAA ACE RB	AG, IN, PW	AG, EN, EP	AGR, ENER
Flood damage. See Disaster relief					
Flowers. See Horticulture					
Food distribution (13, 18)	AGR AGR	FAS FNS	AG, ED	AG	AGR
Food inspection (11)	AGR COM HHS	FSIS NOAA FDA	AG, EN	AG, LA	AGR
Food production. See Agricultural production					
Food stamps (12)	AGR	FNS	AG	AG	AGR
Foreclosure (9, 14)	AGR HUD HUD HUD	FAHA FEHO MHP SHP	AG, BA	AG, BA	AGR, VA

	Parent Agencies	Agency Subunits	House Committees	Senate Committees	Appropriations Subcommittees
Foreign agents (13, 14)	JUS	CRID	JU	FR	COM
Foreign aid (13)	AGR STA TRE IDCA	FAS IFD DNO AID	FA	FR	COM, FA
Foreign currency (9, 13)	TRE FRB	IMA	BA	BA	TRE
Foreign debts. See International finance					
Foreign investments. See International trade					
Foreign property (13)	TRE	FACO	FA	FR	TRE
Foreign residents. See Aliens					
Foreign service. See Diplomatic service					
Foreign sovereign immunity (13, 14)	STA	LAO	JU	JU	COM
Foreign taxes (9, 13)	TRE TRE	INTA IRS	WM	FI	TRE
Foreign visitors (13)	JUS STA USIA	INS CAB	FA, JU	FR, JU	COM
Forestry (16)	AGR INT TVA	FS LMB	AG, IN	AG, EN	INT
Forfeiture. See Criminal procedure					
Forged documents. See Identity papers					
Foster care. See Family services					
Foundations. See Nonprofit organizations					
Franchises (2)	COM FTC SBA	IEB	EN, SB	CO, SB	COM
Fraud. See Consumer protection, Inspectors General, White collar crime					
Freedom of information. See Government information, Privacy, Proprietary data					
Freight (2, 19)	TRA FMC ICC	FAA	MM, PW	CO	COM, TRA

	Parent Agencies	Agency Subunits	House Committees	Senate Committees	Appropriations Subcommittees
Fringe benefits (6, 12)	LAB TRE OPM	PWBA IRS	ED, PO, WM	FI, GA LA	LAB, TRE
Fruits (1, 11)	AGR AGR	AMS FSIS	AG	AG	AGR
Fuel. See Coal, Natural gas, Petroleum					
Funding gaps (9, 10)	TRE EOP	PDB OMB	AP, WM	AP, FI	TRE
Furs. See Endangered species					
Futures markets. See Commodity regulation					
Gambling (14)	JUS JUS JUS	CRID EOUS FBI	JU	JU	COM
Gardening. See Horticulture					
Gas. See Natural gas					
Gasoline. See Petroleum					
Gems. See Precious stones					
Genetics (17)	HHS HHS EOP OTA	NIAI NIGM STP	EN, SC	CO, LA	LAB
Genealogy. See Federal records					
Genocide. See Human rights					
Geography. See Mapping					
Geology (16, 17)	INT NSF SI	GS	IN, SC	CO, EN	INT
Geothermal energy. See Energy research					
Gerontology. See Aged					
Gold. See Precious metals					
Government borrowing (9, 10)	TRE TRE TRE	DFO FFB PDB	WM	FI	TRE
Government contracts (10, 15)	DEF DEF LAB LAB GAO SBA	DCAA DLA ESA FECC	AR, BA, ED, GO, SB	AR, BA, GA, LA, SB	DEF, LAB
Government corporations (10)	GAO		GO	GA	COM, VA

	Parent Agencies	Agency Subunits	House Committees	Senate Committees	Appropriations Subcommittees
Government employees (6, 10)	FLRA MSPB OPM SCO		PO	GA	TRE
Government ethics (10, 14)	OPM		JU, PO	GA, JU	TRE
Government fellowships (5)	EDU NFAH NSF SI	PE	ED	LA	LAB
Government information (3, 10)	DEF JUS EOP GSA GSA	DIS LIA OMB ISO IRMS	GO, JU	GA, JU	COM, TRE
Government liability (14)	JUS GAO	LIA	JU	JU	COM
Government litigation (14)	JUS JUS JUS	EOUS JSB SG	JU	JU	COM
Government procurement (10)	DEF DEF EOP GSA	DLA REO FPP APO	AR, GO, PO	AR, GA	DEF, TRE
Government publications (3, 10)	COM GPO	NTIS	EN, HA (JCP)	CO, RU	LEG
Government securities (9, 10)	TRE TRE TRE FRB	EPB PDB SBD	BA, WM	BA, FI	TRE
Government spending (9, 10)	TRE EOP CBO GAO	FMS OMB	AP, BU, GO	AP, BU, GA	TRE
Grains (1)	AGR AGR AGR	AMS ASCS FGIS	AG	AG	AGR
Grazing lands (16)	INT	LMB	AG, IN	AG, EN	INT
Greenhouse effect. See Atmosphere					
Gross National Product (2, 9)	COM EOP	EAB CEA	BA (JEC)	BA	COM
Ground transportation (2, 17, 19)	TRA ICC	FEHA	EN, PW, SC	CO, EP	TRA
Guns. See Firearms					
Habeus corpus. See Federal courts					
Handicapped (11, 12, 18)	EDU HHS HHS	SERS DDA SSA	ED, EN, SC, WM	FI, LA	LAB

	Parent Agencies	Agency Subunits	House Committees	Senate Committees	Appropriations Subcommittees
Harbors (2, 4, 19)	COM TRA TRA FMC	NOAA CG MA	MM, PW	CO, EN, EP	COM, TRA
Hazardous materials (8, 11)	LAB TRA TRA CPSC EPA NTSB	OSHA FEHA HMT	EN, PW	CO, EP	TRA, VA
Headaches. See Neurological diseases					
Health care (11)	HHS HHS HHS HHS VA OTA	HCD HFB HPB NCHSR VHSRA	EN, VA	LA, VA	LAB, VA
Health data (11)	LAB HHS HHS	LSB NCHS PHS	EN	LA	LAB
Health education. See Preventive medicine					
Health insurance (9, 11)	HHS CBO OPM	HCFA	EN, PO, WM	FI, GA, LA	LAB, TRE
Health maintenance organizations (11)	HHS HHS HHS	HCFA HMO HRSA	EN, PO, WM	FI, GA, LA	LAB
Heart disease (11)	HHS HHS	NHL NINC	EN	LA	LAB
Helicopters. See Aviation safety					
Herbicides (1, 8, 11)	AGR AGR HHS EPA	ARS FS FDA	AG, EN, SC	AG, CO, EP	AGR, VA
High schools. See Secondary education					
Higher education (5)	EDU	PE	ED	LA	LAB
Highway construction (4, 19)	TRA	FEHA	PW	EP	TRA
Highway safety (11, 17, 19)	TRA TRA TRA NTSB	FEHA MCS NHTSA	EN, PW, SC	CO, EP	TRA
Hijacking (14, 19)	JUS TRA	FBI CAS	JU	JU	COM, TRA
Historic preservation (5, 16)	INT NCPC PADC SI	NPS	BA, HA, IN	EN, RU	INT

	Parent Agencies	Agency Subunits	House Committees	Senate Committees	Appropriations Subcommittees
Historical documents. See Federal records					
Holidays (10)	OPM		JU, PO	JU	TRE
Home building. See Housing industry					
Home economics (5)	AGR EDU	ES VAE	AG, ED	AG, LA	AGR, LAB
Home entertainment. See Recording industry					
Home mortgages. See Mortgage loans					
Homelessness (12, 18, 20)	EDU HHS HHS HUD HUD FEMA	VAE HCFA SSA CPD MHP	BA, ED, EN, GO,	BA, FI, GA, LA	LAB, VA
Homesteading (20)	HUD HUD	UHO URO	BA	BA	VA
Horticulture (1)	AGR AGR SI	APHIS NA	AG	AG	AGR
Hospice care. See Hospital facilities					
Hospital facilities (11)	HHS	HRSA	EN	LA	LAB
Hospital regulation (11, 18)	HHS VA	HCFA VHSRA	EN, VA	LA, VA	LAB, VA
Hostages. See Terrorism					
House of Representatives. See Congressional operations					
Housing data. See Census					
Housing industry (9, 20)	HUD HUD	CPD PDR	BA (JEC)	BA	VA
Housing management (12, 20)	HUD HUD	FEHO MHP	BA	BA	VA
Human rights (13)	STA STA SCEC	HRHA IOA	FA	FR	COM, FA
Humanities (5)	NFAH SI		ED, HA	LA, RU	INT
Hunger (13, 18)	AGR AGR	FAS FNS	AG, ED, FA	AG, FR, LA	AGR
Hunting. See Wildlife conservation					
Hurricanes. See Disaster relief					

	Parent Agencies	Agency Subunits	House Committees	Senate Committees	Appropriations Subcommittees
Hydroelectric power (7, 8)	ENER INT	FERC RB	EN, IN	EN	ENER
Identity papers (10, 14)	JUS TRE	INS SS	GO	GA	COM, TRE
Illiteracy. See Literacy					
Immigration (13, 14)	JUS STA	INS CAB	JU	JU	COM
Immunization (11)	HHS	CDC	EN	LA	LAB
Impeachment (10, 14)	JUS	CRID	JU	JU	COM, LEG
Imports (2, 13)	COM COM STA TRE ITC	FTZB IMP EBA CS	EN, FA, WM	CO, FI, FR	COM
Impoundments (9, 10)	EOP GAO	OMB	AP, RU	AP, RU	TRE
Income tax. See Taxation					
Indians (16, 18)	EDU HHS HHS HUD INT JUS SI	INED IHS NAA IHO IAB LNR	IN	IN	INT, LAB
Individual retirement accounts (9)	TRE	IRS	BA, WM	BA, FI	TRE
Industrial pollution (8, 11)	EOP EPA OTA	STP	EN	EN, EP	VA
Industrial relations. See Labor relations					
Industrial safety. See Occupational safety					
Industrial surveys. See Economic data					
Industrial technology (2, 17)	COM COM EOP NSF OTA SBA	NIST PTI STP	EN, SB, SC (JEC)	CO, SB	COM, VA
Infant mortality (11)	HHS	NICH	EN	LA	LAB
Infectious diseases. See Communicable diseases					
Inflation. See Economic data					
Influenza. See Communicable diseases					

	Parent Agencies	Agency Subunits	House Committees	Senate Committees	Appropriations Subcommittees
Information management. See Federal paperwork, Government information, Public administration					
Information resources. See Libraries					
Information science. See Computer technology					
Injunctions. See Judicial remedies					
Inland waterways (2, 4, 16, 19)	DEF TRA TRA ICC	ACE CG MA	EN, IN, PW	CO, EN, EP	COM, TRA
Insects (1, 16)	AGR AGR SI	APHIS ARS	AG	AG	AGR
Inspectors General (10)	EOP GAO	OMB	GO	GA	TRE
Insurance industry (2)	FRB FTC		BA, EN	BA, JU	COM
Insurance programs (4, 12, 20)	HUD VA FEMA SBA	FEHO VBA	BA, SB, VA	BA, SB, VA	VA
Intellectual property. See Copyrights					
Intelligence activities (13, 15)	DEF DEF JUS STA EOP	DIA IOO IPR IRB CIA	AR, FA, INT	AR, FR, INT	DEF
Interagency relations (10)	EOP GAO	OMB	GO	GA	TRE
Interest rates (2, 9)	TRE TRE FRB	DFO PDB	BA, WM (JEC)	BA, FI	TRE, VA
Intergovernmental relations (10, 20)	EOP ACIR GAO	OMB	GO	GA	TRE
International agreements (13, 15)	STA STA STA STA STA STA	CAB EBA ECA IOA LAO PMA	FA	FR	COM
International arbitration (13)	STA USIP	FSE	FA	FR	COM
International boundaries (13)	STA	IRB	FA	FR	COM
International claims (13, 14)	JUS STA	FCSC LAO	FA	FR	COM

	Parent Agencies	Agency Subunits	House Committees	Senate Committees	Appropriations Subcommittees
International communication (2, 3, 13)	STA STA TRE FCC IBB USIA	EBA ICIP CS	EN, FA	CO, FR	COM
International crime (13, 14)	JUS JUS STA STA	DEA INTER INM LEI	FA, JU	FR, JU	COM
International finance (9, 13)	COM STA TRE EXIM FRB IDCA SEC	IEP IFD IAO OPIC	BA, FA, WM	BA, FI, FR	COM, FA
International law (13, 14)	JUS STA	CID LAO	FA	FR	COM
International organizations (13)	STA TRE	IOA IAO	BA, FA	BA, FR	FA
International trade (2, 13)	AGR COM COM COM LAB STA TRA TRE EOP FMC IDCA ITC SBA	FAS FTZB IEP ITA ILA EBA MA TIP TRO TDP	AG, BA, EN, FA, MM, SB, WM (JEC)	AG, BA, CO, FI, FR, SB	COM, FA
International transportation (2, 13)	STA TRA FMC	EBA IAV	EN, FA, MM, PW	CO, EP, FR	COM, TRA
International travel (13)	COM STA USIA	TTA CAB	EN, FA	CO, FR	COM
International waters (13, 15)	DEF STA STA TRA	NAVY LAO OIE CG	FA, MM	CO, FR	COM
Interstate relations (10, 14)	JUS	LIA	EN, JU	CO, JU	COM

Intervention abroad. See
  National security

Inventions. See Patents

Investment companies. See
  Securities industry

	Parent Agencies	Agency Subunits	House Committees	Senate Committees	Appropriations Subcommittees
Irrigation (1, 16)	AGR INT TVA	SCS RB	AG, IN	AG, EN	AGR, ENER

	Parent Agencies	Agency Subunits	House Committees	Senate Committees	Appropriations Subcommittees
Job training. See Apprenticeship, Vocational rehabilitation, Welfare					
Journalistic confidentiality (3, 14)	JUS	CID	JU	JU	COM
Judicial administration (10, 14)	JUS	JMD	JU	JU	COM
Judicial ethics (14)	JUS	AG	JU	JU	COM
Judicial power. See Federal courts					
Judicial remedies (14)	JUS JUS	LIA SG	JU	JU	COM
Juries (14)	JUS	LIA	JU	JU	COM
Juvenile delinquency (5, 14)	EDU HHS JUS JUS	CEP CYFA JJDP NIJ	ED, JU	JU, LA	COM, LAB
Labor relations (6)	LAB FLRA FMCS NLRB NMB OPM	LMR	ED, GO, PO (JEC)	GA, LA	LAB, TRE
Labor standards (6)	LAB LAB	ESA LMS	ED	LA	LAB
Laboratory research (17)	COM NSF OTA	NIST	SC	CO	COM
Lakes. See Inland waterways					
Land management (1, 16)	AGR AGR HUD INT INT	FS SCS EEO LMB NPS	AG, BA, IN	AG, BA, EN	INT
Land sales (2, 4, 20)	HUD FTC	ILS	BA	BA	VA
Languages. See Humanities					
Law enforcement (14)	JUS JUS JUS JUS TRE TRE TRE TRE	EOUS FBI MS NIJ ATF FLET IRS SS	JU	JU	COM, TRE
Learning disabilities (5, 18)	EDU HHS	SERS DDA	ED, EN	LA	LAB
Legal services (14)	LSC		JU	LA	COM
Legal tender. See Currency					

	Parent Agencies	Agency Subunits	House Committees	Senate Committees	Appropriations Subcommittees
Legislative process. See Congressional operations					
Lending. See Credit programs, Financial institutions, Interest rates					
Leukemia. See Blood					
Liability insurance. See Product liability					
Libraries (5)	EDU GPO LC NCLIS	LPD	ED, HA	LA, RU	LAB, LEG
Lie detectors. See Polygraphs					
Life insurance. See Insurance industry					
Life sciences. See Biotechnology, Genetics, Medical research					
Liquor. See Alcoholic beverages					
Literacy (5)	EDU EDU	CEP NIE	ED	LA	LAB
Literature. See Humanities					
Livestock (1)	AGR AGR AGR	AMS APHIS PSA	AG	AG	AGR
Lobbying (10, 14)	JUS TRE	CRID IRS	HA, JU, WM	FI, GA, RU	COM, TRE
Local governments (9, 10, 20)	COM TRE ACIR	CB RSO	GO	GA	COM, TRE
Lockouts. See Labor relations					
Lotteries (2)	JUS FCC PS	CRID	JU, PO	GA, JU	COM
Lumber. See Timber resources					
Magazines. See Copyrights					
Mail delivery. See Postal Service					
Mail order sales. See Consumer protection					
Mapping (10, 16)	COM COM DEF INT EOP	CB NOAA DMA GS CIA	AR, EN, IN	AR, CO, EP	COM, DEF, INT

	Parent Agencies	Agency Subunits	House Committees	Senate Committees	Appropriations Subcommittees
Marihuana. See Drug abuse, Drug testing, Drug traffic					
Marine Corps (15)	DEF	NAVY	AR	AR	DEF
Marine resources (8, 16, 17)	COM INT STA EOP OTA	NOAA FWS OIE STP	IN, MM, SC	CO, EP	COM, INT
Marine safety (6, 11, 19)	LAB TRA NTSB	OSHA CG	MM	CO	TRA
Maritime industry (2, 13, 16)	STA TRA TRA FMC	EBA CG MA	MM	CO	COM, TRA
Martial law. See Military law					
Mass media. See Broadcasting					
Mass transit (19, 20)	TRA NTSB	UMT	PW	BA	TRA
Meat (1, 11)	AGR AGR AGR	AMS FSIS PSA	AG	AG	AGR
Medicaid. See Health insurance					
Medical devices (11, 17)	HHS	FDA	EN	LA	AGR, LAB
Medical insurance. See Health insurance					
Medical malpractice. See Health insurance					
Medical personnel. See Health care					
Medical research (11, 17)	HHS HHS HHS	NCHSR NIH NLM	EN, SC	LA	LAB
Medicare. See Health insurance					
Members of Congress (10)	JUS JUS	CID CRID	HA, ST	ET, RU	LEG
Mental health (11)	HHS	NIMH	EN	LA	LAB
Mental illness. See Handicapped					
Merchant marine. See Maritime industry					
Metals. See Mining industry					
Meteorology. See Weather					

	Parent Agencies	Agency Subunits	House Committees	Senate Committees	Appropriations Subcommittees
Metric system. See Weights and measures					
Metropolitan areas. See Local governments					
Migrant workers (6, 18)	EDU HHS LAB LAB	CEP HRSA ESA ETA	ED	LA	LAB
Military assistance (13, 15)	DEF DEF STA EOP	DSA ISA PMA NSC	AR, FA	AR, FR	DEF, FA
Military education. See Service academies					
Military installations (4, 15)	DEF	INST	AR	AR	MC
Military law (13, 15)	DEF STA EOP	JCS PMA NSC	AR, FA	AR, FR	DEF
Military operations (15)	DEF DEF	CCCI JCS	AR	AR	DEF
Military personnel (15)	DEF	FMP	AR	AR	DEF
Military research (15, 17)	DEF DEF DEF OTA	DAR DLA REO	AR	AR	DEF
Military reserves. See National Guard					
Military strategy. See National security					
Milk. See Dairy industry					
Mine safety (6, 11)	INT LAB FMSH	MB MSHA	ED	LA	INT, LAB
Mineral leases (2, 7, 16)	COM INT INT	NOAA LMB MMS	IN, MM	EN	COM, INT
Mineral resources (8, 16)	INT INT INT EOP OTA	GS LMB MB STP	IN, SC	EN	INT
Minimum wage. See Wages					
Mining industry (2, 8)	INT INT EPA	MB SMRE	EN, IN	EN	INT, VA
Minorities. See Civil rights					
Mismanagement. See Inspectors General					

	Parent Agencies	Agency Subunits	House Committees	Senate Committees	Appropriations Subcommittees
National libraries. See Agricultural research, Libraries, Medical research					
National security (13, 15)	DEF DEF DEF DEF ENER STA EOP OTA	DIS ISP JCS NSA IAE PMA NSC	AR, FA	AR, FR	COM, DEF
National wealth. See Gross National Product					
Native Americans. See Indians					
Natural disasters. See Disaster relief					
Natural gas (7, 16)	ENER ENER INT	ERA FEO MMS	EN, SC	CO, EN	INT
Naturalization (10, 14)	JUS	INS	JU	JU	COM
Navigable waters. See Inland waterways					
Navy. See Armed forces					
Neglect of duty. See Inspectors General					
Negotiable instruments (2, 9)	FRB SEC		BA, EN	BA	COM, TRE
Neurological diseases (11)	HHS	NINC	EN	LA	LAB
Neuroses. See Mental health					
Neutrality law (13, 14)	COM JUS STA STA TRE	ITA CRID EBA LAO CS	FA	FR	COM
Newspapers. See Journalistic confidentiality					
Noise pollution (8, 17)	EPA		EN, SC	CO, EP	VA
Nominations. See Presidency					
Nonprofit organizations (3, 5)	TRE NFAH PS	IRS	WM	FI	TRE
Nuclear energy (7, 16, 17)	ENER ENER ENER EOP OTA	ERA FERC NEO STP	AR, EN, IN, SC	AR, EN, EP, GA	ENER
Nuclear facilities (7, 8)	ENER NRC	ESH	EN, IN	EP, GA	ENER

	Parent Agencies	Agency Subunits	House Committees	Senate Committees	Appropriations Subcommittees
Nuclear proliferation (13, 15)	DEF ENER STA EOP ACDA	ISP INN PMA NSC	AR, FA	AR, FR, GA	COM, DEF
Nuclear safety (8, 11)	ENER FEMA NRC	ESH	EN, IN	EN, EP	ENER
Nuclear testing (15, 17)	DEF ENER ACDA	DNA DPO	AR, FA	AR, FR	DEF, ENER
Nuclear waste (8, 17)	ENER ENER ENER EOP NRC OTA	CRW DPO RAW STP	EN, IN, SC	EN, EP, GA	ENER
Numismatics (2, 5)	TRE	MINT	BA	BA	TRE
Nursing homes (11, 18)	HHS HUD	HCFA MHP	BA, EN, WM	BA, FI, LA	LAB
Nutrition (5, 11)	AGR AGR HHS HHS	FNS HNIS FDA NIDD	AG, ED, EN, SC	AG, LA	AGR
Obscenity (3, 14)	JUS FCC PS	CRID	JU	JU	COM
Occupational safety (6, 11)	HHS LAB OSHR	NIOS OSHA	ED, PO, SB	GA, LA, SB	LAB
Ocean liners. See Passenger ships					
Ocean use (8, 13, 16, 19)	COM DEF STA TRA	NOAA ISA OIE MA	FA, MM, SC	CO, EP, FR	COM, DEF
Oceanography (8, 16, 17)	COM DEF NSF OTA	NOAA NRO	MM, SC	CO	COM, DEF
Offshore drilling (7, 17)	COM ENER INT NSF	NOAA FERC MMS	EN, IN, MM	CO, EN	ENER, INT
Oil. See Petroleum					
Oil spills (8, 19)	TRA EPA NTSB	CG	EN, MM, PW	CO, EP	TRA, VA
Olympic games. See Sports					
Organ transplants (11, 17)	HHS	MCHRD	EN	LA	LAB

	Parent Agencies	Agency Subunits	House Committees	Senate Committees	Appropriations Subcommittees
Organized crime (14)	JUS JUS JUS	CRID EOUS FBI	JU	GA, JU	COM
Orphans. See Family services					
Outdoor recreation. See Recreation areas					
Outer continental shelf (7, 16)	INT INT	GS MMS	IN, MM	CO, EN	INT
Ozone layer. See Atmosphere					
Panama Canal (2, 13, 15)	STA PCC	IAA	MM	AR, CO	COM, TRA
Pardons (14)	JUS	PAO	JU	JU	COM
Parks. See Recreation areas					
Parole (14)	JUS	PC	JU	JU	COM
Passenger ships (2, 19)	TRA FMC	CG	MM	CO	COM, TRA
Passports. See International travel					
Patents (14, 17)	COM STA	PTO EBA	JU, SC	CO, JU	COM
Peacekeeping forces. See Military assistance					
Pediatrics. See Child health					
Pensions (6, 9, 10, 12)	LAB VA CBO OPM PBGC	PWBA VBA	ED, PO, VA	GA, LA, VA	LAB, TRE, VA
Performing arts. See Arts					

Personal finance. See Bank
  deposits, Bankruptcy, Con-
  sumer credit, Individual
  retirement accounts, Mort-
  gage loans, Pensions					

Pesticides (1, 8, 11)	AGR HHS EPA	ARS FDA	AG, EN	AG, LA	AGR, VA
Petroleum (7, 8, 16)	ENER ENER INT	FEO FERC MMS	EN, IN, SC	EN	ENER, INT
Pharmaceutical industry. See Drug safety					
Philanthropy. See Charitable organizations					
Philately (2, 5)	TRE PS	EPB	GO, PO	GA	TRE

	Parent Agencies	Agency Subunits	House Committees	Senate Committees	Appropriations Subcommittees
Phobias. See Mental health					
Physical disability. See Handicapped					
Physical education (5, 11)	HHS	PHS	EN	LA	LAB
Physical security (10)	INT TRE GSA	NPS SS PBS	GO, HA	GA, RU	TRE
Pipelines (2, 7, 8, 17)	ENER TRA NTSB	FERC PSO	EN, IN, PW	CO, EN	ENER, TRA
Plants (1, 16)	AGR AGR SI	APHIS ARS	AG	AG	AGR
Plastics (2, 17)	COM CPSC NSF	NIST	EN, SC	CO	COM, VA
Poisons. See Toxic substances					
Polar regions (13, 17)	STA NSF	OIE	FA, SC	CO, FR	COM, VA
Police forces. See Border patrol, Law enforcement, Physical security					
Political activities. See Government employees					
Political asylum (10, 13)	JUS STA	INS HRHA	FA, JU	FR, JU	COM
Political contributions. See Elections					
Political expression. See Advertising, Lobbying, Public demonstrations					
Pollution. See Acid rain, Air pollution, Industrial pollution, Noise pollution, Waste management, Water pollution					
Polygraphs (6, 14)	DEF JUS JUS LAB OPM OTA	DIS LIA NIJ ESA	ED, JU, PO	GA, JU, LA	COM, LAB, TRE
Population data. See Census					
Population growth (8, 11, 13)	COM HHS STA IDCA	CB NICH OIE AID	EN, FA	FR, LA	FA, LAB
Pornography (14)	JUS PS	CRID	JU	JU	COM
Ports. See Harbors					

	Parent Agencies	Agency Subunits	House Committees	Senate Committees	Appropriations Subcommittees
Postal Service (2, 10)	PRC PS		GO, PO	GA	TRE
Poultry (1)	AGR AGR AGR AGR	AMS APHIS FSIS PSA	AG	AG	AGR
Poverty level. See Census					
Poverty programs. See Food stamps, Homelessness, Welfare					
Power failures. See Energy consumption					
Precious metals (2, 9, 16)	INT TRE CFTC FRB	MB MINT	BA	BA	INT, TRE
Precious stones (2, 16)	COM INT ITC SI	ITA MB	EN, WM	CO, FI	COM, INT
Prenatal care (11, 18)	HHS HHS	NICH PHS	ED	LA	LAB
Preschool education (5)	EDU HHS	ESE HB	ED	LA	LAB
Presidency (10)	JUS TRE EOP FEC	AG SS WHO	GO, HA, JU	GA, JU, RU	COM, TRE
Preventive medicine (5, 11)	HHS HHS HHS	CDC NCHSR NIH	EN	LA	LAB
Price controls. See Economic controls					
Price supports. See Agricultural subsidies					
Prices. See Consumer Price Index					
Printing. See Government publications					
Prisoners (14)	JUS JUS JUS JUS	JAB NIJ PB PC	JU	JU	COM
Prisons. See Correctional facilities					
Privacy (3, 14, 17)	DEF JUS EOP EOP NARA OTA	DPB LIA OMB STP	GO, JU, SC	CO, GA, JU	COM, TRE

	Parent Agencies	Agency Subunits	House Committees	Senate Committees	Appropriations Subcommittees
Private property. See Eminent domain					
Private schools (5)	EDU EDU EDU	ESE PE PRE	ED	LA	LAB
Probation. See Sentences					
Product labeling (2, 11)	HHS TRE CPSC FTC	FDA ATF	EN	CO	COM, VA
Product liability (2)	JUS CPSC	CID	EN, JU	CO, JU	COM, VA
Product safety (11, 17)	COM HHS CPSC FTC	NIST FDA	EN	CO	COM, VA
Productivity. See Gross National Product					
Property insurance. See Insurance industry					
Proprietary data (2, 3)	ENER JUS FTC SEC	FERC LIA	EN	CO	COM, ENER
Protectionism. See International trade					
Public administration (10)	EOP ACUS GAO GSA NARA OPM	OMB	GO, PO	GA	TRE
Public broadcasting (3, 5)	COM FCC NFAH	NTIA	EN	CO	COM
Public buildings (4, 10)	FAC GSA NCPC NFAH	PBS	PW	EP, GA	INT, TRE
Public debt (9, 10)	TRE TRE EOP CBO	FFB PDB OMB	BU, WM (JEC)	BU, FI	TRE
Public demonstrations (3, 14)	INT JUS	NPS MS	JU	JU	COM, INT
Public domain. See Government information					
Public finance. See Budget deficits, Budget formulation, Government borrowing, Government spending, Public debt, Taxation					

	Parent Agencies	Agency Subunits	House Committees	Senate Committees	Appropriations Subcommittees
Public housing (4, 20)	HUD	PHO	BA	BA	VA
Public lands (8, 16)	AGR INT INT	FS LMB NPS	IN	EN	INT
Public officials. See Federal judges, Government employees, Members of Congress					
Public schools (5)	EDU EDU	ESE PE	ED	LA	LAB
Public utilities (7, 8)	ENER NRC TVA	FERC	EN, IN, PW	EN, EP	ENER
Purchasing power. See Consumer Price Index					
Quotas. See Agricultural production, Immigration, Imports					
Radiation (6, 8, 11, 17)	COM ENER HHS LAB EOP EPA NRC OTA	NIST ESH FDA OSHA STP	ED, EN, IN, SC	CO, EP, LA	ENER, LAB, VA
Radio industry. See Broadcasting					
Radioactive waste. See Nuclear waste					
Radioactivity. See Nuclear safety					
Radon (8, 11)	EPA		EN	EP	VA
Railroad industry (2, 19)	TRA ICC	FRA	EN	CO	TRA
Railroad safety (11, 17, 19)	TRA NTSB	FRA	EN	CO	TRA
Real estate industry (4, 9, 20)	HUD TRE	FEHO IRS	BA, WM	BA, FI	VA
Recession. See Economic data					
Reclamation. See Land management					
Reconciliation. See Budget formulation					
Recording industry (2, 3, 14, 17)	CRT FCC		EN, JU	CO, JU	COM
Records management. See Federal paperwork					

	Parent Agencies	Agency Subunits	House Committees	Senate Committees	Appropriations Subcommittees
Recreation areas (8, 16)	AGR INT INT INT INT TVA	FS FWS LMB NPS RB	IN	EN	INT
Recycling. See Waste management					
Red tape. See Federal paperwork					
Refugees (13, 14, 18)	HHS JUS JUS STA	RRO CORS INS RPB	ED, FA, JU	FR, JU, LA	COM, LAB
Regulatory procedure. See Administrative law					
Rehabilitation services (5, 11, 18)	EDU HHS VA	SERS DDA VHSRA	ED, EN, VA	LA, VA	LAB, VA
Religious institutions (3, 18)	JUS TRE	CID IRS	JU, WM	FI, JU	COM
Remedial instruction. See Compensatory education					
Rent control. See Economic controls					
Rental housing. See Housing management					
Repatriation (13)	STA	RPB	FA	FR	COM

Representation. See
  Congressional districts,
  Elections, Voting					

Representatives. See Members of Congress					
Rescissions. See Impoundments					
Reservoirs. See Water supply					
Resource shortages (2, 7, 13, 16)	COM ENER INT TRE	ITA IAE MB TIP	EN, IN	CO, EN	COM, ENER
Respiratory diseases (11)	HHS HHS	NHL NIAI	EN	EP, LA	LAB
Retail trade. See Economic data					
Retirement (6, 12, 18)	HHS LAB TRE OPM	SSA PWBA IRS	ED, PO, WM	FI, GA, LA	LAB, TRE
Revenue. See Taxation					

	Parent Agencies	Agency Subunits	House Committees	Senate Committees	Appropriations Subcommittees
Revenue sharing (9, 10)	COM TRE	CB RSO	GO, WM	FI, GA	TRE
Rights-of-way (8, 19)	INT TRA TRA	LMB FEHA FRA	IN	EN	INT, TRA

Riots. See Civil disorders

Rivers. See Inland waterways

Robotics. See Industrial technology

Runaways. See Missing children

	Parent Agencies	Agency Subunits	House Committees	Senate Committees	Appropriations Subcommittees
Rural areas (1, 2, 4)	AGR AGR AGR SBA	FAHA RDP REA	AG, SB	AG, SB	AGR

Sabotage. See Subversive activities

Saline water. See Water supply

Salt. See Nutrition

Salvage. See Maritime industry

Sanitation. See Waste management

Satellites. See Space communication

Savings and loan associations. See Financial institutions

Savings bonds. See Government securities

Scenic areas. See Wilderness areas

Scholarships. See Government fellowships

Scientific research. See Agricultural research, Energy research, Environmental research, Laboratory research, Medical research, Military research

Seabed mining. See Undersea exploration

	Parent Agencies	Agency Subunits	House Committees	Senate Committees	Appropriations Subcommittees
Seal of the U.S. (10, 14)	STA	SOS	JU	JU	COM

Searches and seizures. See Law enforcement

Seashores. See Recreation areas

	Parent Agencies	Agency Subunits	House Committees	Senate Committees	Appropriations Subcommittees
Secondary education (5)	EDU	ESE	ED	LA	LAB
Securities industry (2, 9)	TRE FRB SEC	FIP	BA, EN	BA	COM, TRE
Seeds. See Agricultural research, Horticulture, Plants					
Selective Service (15)	SSS		AR	AR	VA
Self-employment. See Taxation					
Senate. See Congressional operations					
Senators. See Members of Congress					
Senior citizens. See Aged					
Senior Executive Service. See Government employees					
Sentences (14)	JUS	SC	JU	JU	COM
Separation of powers (10, 14)	JUS LC	AG CRS	GO, JU	GA, JU	COM, LEG
Service academies (5, 15)	DEF DEF DEF TRA TRA	AF ARMY NAVY CG MA	AR, MM	AR, CO	DEF, TRA
Sewage treatment. See Waste management					
Shipping. See Maritime industry					
Shoreline erosion. See Coastal zone management					
Shoreline patrol. See Territorial waters					
Silver. See Precious metals					
Skin diseases (11)	HHS	NIAM	EN	LA	LAB
Sleep disorders. See Mental health					
Slum clearance (20)	HUD HUD	PDR UDAG	BA	BA	VA
Small business (2, 4, 20)	COM FEMA GSA SBA	MBDA SDB	SB (JEC)	SB	COM
Smoking (11)	HHS HHS HHS	NCI NHL SHO	EN	LA	LAB

	Parent Agencies	Agency Subunits	House Committees	Senate Committees	Appropriations Subcommittees
Smuggling (14)	JUS TRA TRA TRE	INS CG FAA CS	FA, JU	FR, JU	COM, TRE
Social sciences (5)	NSF		SC	LA	VA
Social Security (9, 12, 18)	HHS	SSA	BU, WM	BU, FI	LAB
Socioeconomic data. See Census					
Software industry. See Computer security, Computer technology, Copyrights					
Soil conservation (1, 16, 17)	AGR	SCS	AG	AG	AGR
Solar energy. See Energy research					
Solid waste. See Waste management					
Sovereign immunity. See Government liability					
Space commercialization (2, 17)	COM TRA NASA	SOC CST	SC	CO	TRA, VA
Space communication (3, 15, 17)	DEF FCC NASA	DCA	AR, EN, SC	AR, CO	COM, VA
Space exploration (10, 17)	EOP NASA OTA SI	STP	SC	CO	INT, VA
Special education. See Handicapped, Learning disabilities, Rehabilitation services					
Sports (2, 5)	EDU FTC	PE	ED, EN	CO, LA	COM, LAB
Spying. See Espionage					
Stamps. See Philately					
Standard of living. See Economic data					
Standard time. See Time zones					
State boundaries (10)	INT JUS	GS LIA	JU	JU	COM
State governments (9, 10)	COM TRE ACIR	CB RSO	GO	GA	TRE
Stock markets. See Securities industry					
Storms. See Disaster relief, Insurance industry, Weather					

	Parent Agencies	Agency Subunits	House Committees	Senate Committees	Appropriations Subcommittees
Strategic stockpiles (15, 16)	COM DEF ENER STA FEMA GSA OTA	SRO DLA DPO EBA FPR	AR, SC	AR	COM, DEF TRE
Strikes. See Labor relations					
Student loans (5, 9)	EDU HHS	PE HPB	ED	LA	LAB
Subsidized housing. See Housing management, Mortgage loans, Public housing					
Subversive activities (14, 15)	JUS JUS JUS	CRID FBI INTER	JU	JU	COM
Subways. See Mass transit					
Sugar (1, 11)	AGR AGR HHS CFTC	ASCS HNIS FDA	AG	AG	AGR
Suicide. See Mental health					
Supply and demand. See Economic data					
Supreme Court. See Federal courts					
Synthetic fuels. See Energy research					
Tariffs (2, 9, 13)	COM TRE EOP ITC	IMP CS TRO	WM (JEC)	FI	COM, TRE
Taxation (9, 10)	TRE TRE EOP CBO	IRS TPO CEA	BU, WM (JEC)	BU, FI	TRE
Technological risk (17)	EOP NSF OTA	STP	SC	CO	VA
Technology transfer (2, 8, 13, 17)	COM DEF STA TRE EPA	EXP DTSA OIE TIP	EN, SC	CO	COM, DEF
Telecommunications (2, 3, 17)	COM DEF EOP FCC OTA	NTIA DCA STP	AR, EN, SC	AR, CO	COM
Telephone service. See Telecommunications					

	Parent Agencies	Agency Subunits	House Committees	Senate Committees	Appropriations Subcommittees
Television industry. See Broadcasting					
Tenants. See Housing management					
Territorial waters (8, 15)	COM JUS TRA	NOAA LNR CG	MM	CO	COM, TRA
Territories (10)	INT STA	TIA PIA	IN	EN	COM, INT
Terrorism (13, 14, 15)	JUS JUS STA EOP	FBI INTER DSB NSC	FA, JU	FR, JU	COM
Thrift industry. See Financial institutions					
Timber resources (8, 16)	AGR INT	FS LMB	AG, IN	AG, EN	INT
Time zones (19)	TRA	SOT	EN	CO	TRA
Tobacco industry (1, 14)	AGR AGR TRE TRE	AMS ASCS ATF IRS	AG, EN, WM	AG, CO, FI	AGR, TRE
Tornadoes. See Disaster relief					
Topography. See Mapping					
Torts. See Government liability					
Torture victims. See Human rights					
Tourism (2)	COM	TTA	EN	CO	COM
Toxic substances (8, 11)	HHS HHS LAB CPSC EPA	FDA TSDR OSHA	EN, SC	EP, LA	LAB, VA
Toys. See Product safety					
Trade secrets. See Proprietary data					
Trademarks (2, 14)	COM STA	PTO EBA	JU	JU	COM
Traffic accidents. See Highway safety					
Trains. See Railroad industry					
Trash. See Waste management					
Travel industry. See Tourism					
Treason (13, 14)	JUS	FBI	JU	JU	COM

	Parent Agencies	Agency Subunits	House Committees	Senate Committees	Appropriations Subcommittees
Treasury securities. See Government securities					
Treaties (13, 14, 15)	JUS STA	AG TAO	FA	FR	COM
Trees. See Forestry					
Trials (14)	JUS JUS	EOUS LIA	JU	JU	COM
Tribal rights. See Indians					
Trucking industry (2, 19)	ICC		EN, PW	CO	TRA
Trust funds (9, 18)	TRE CBO	FMS	BU, WM	BU, FI	TRE
Tuition. See Student loans					
Tunnels (4, 19)	TRA TRA	FEHA FRA	PW	EP	TRA
Undersea exploration (16, 17)	COM DEF STA EOP NSF OTA	NOAA NRO OIE STP	MM	CO, EN	COM, VA
Unemployment compensation (6, 12)	LAB	ETA	WM	FI	LAB
Unemployment rate (6)	LAB	LSB	ED (JEC)	LA	LAB
Unions. See Labor relations					
United Nations. See International organizations					
Universities. See Higher education					
Uranium. See Nuclear energy					
Vaccination. See Immunization					
Vegetables. See Fruits					
Venereal disease (11)	HHS HHS	CDC NIAI	EN	LA	LAB
Vessels. See Maritime industry					
Veterans (5, 6, 11)	EDU LAB VA VA OPM SBA	VPO VETS VBA VHSRA	VA	VA	LAB, VA
Veterinary medicine. See Animals					
Vice-Presidency (10)	JUS TRE FEC	AG SS	GO, HA, JU	GA, JU, RU	COM, TRE

	Parent Agencies	Agency Subunits	House Committees	Senate Committees	Appropriations Subcommittees
Video equipment. See Recording industry					
Violent crime (14)	JUS JUS JUS	EOUS FBI NIJ	JU	JU	COM
Visas. See International travel					
Visual arts. See Arts					
Visual disorders (11)	EDU HHS HHS	SERS NEI SSA	EN	LA	LAB
Vital records. See Privacy					
Vitamins. See Nutrition					
Vocational education (5, 6)	EDU VA	VAE VBA	ED, VA	LA, VA	LAB, VA
Vocational rehabilitation (6, 18)	EDU LAB VA EEOC	SERS ESA VBA	ED, EN, VA	LA, VA	LAB, VA
Volcanoes. See Geology					
Volunteer services (5, 13)	ACTION PCO	VISTA	ED, FA	FR, LA	FA, LAB
Voting (10, 14)	JUS CRC	CRD	JU	JU	COM
Wage controls. See Economic controls					
Wages (6)	DEF LAB LAB LAB EEOC OPM	FMP ESA LSB WIR	AR, ED, PO	AR, GA, (JEC) LA	LAB, TRE
War powers (10, 13, 14)	JUS EOP LC	AG NSC CRS	FA	FR	COM, LEG
Warfare (13, 15)	DEF STA EOP	ISP PMA NSC	AR, FA	AR, FR	COM, DEF
Warranties. See Consumer protection					
Washington, D.C. See District of Columbia					
Waste management (4, 8, 17, 20)	HUD EOP EPA OTA	EEO STP	EN, PW, SC	EP	VA
Water pollution (8, 16, 17)	COM EPA	NOAA	EN, IN, MM, PW, SC	CO, EP	COM, VA

	Parent Agencies	Agency Subunits	House Committees	Senate Committees	Appropriations Subcommittees
Water power (4, 7)	INT TVA	RB	EN, IN, PW	EN, EP	ENER
Water supply (11, 16, 17)	AGR INT INT TVA	SCS GS RB	AG, EN, IN, PW,	AG, EN, EP	ENER, INT
Water transportation (2, 17, 19)	TRA TRA FMC ICC	CG MA	EN, MM, PW, SC	CO, EP	COM, TRA
Weapons (15, 17)	DEF DEF ENER EOP OTA	DNA REO DPO STP	AR	AR	DEF, ENER
Weather (1, 8, 17)	COM NSF OTA	NWS	MM, SC	CO	COM, VA
Weights and measures (2, 17)	COM	NIST	SC	CO	COM
Welfare (9, 12, 18)	HHS HHS LAB	FSA SSA ETA	ED, WM	FI, LA	LAB
Wheat. See Grains					
Whistleblowers. See Government employees					
White collar crime (14)	DEF JUS JUS JUS TRE TRE PS SEC	DIS CID CRID JSB IRS SS	BA, GO, JU	BA, GA, JU	COM, TRE
White House facilities (10)	INT GSA	NPS PBS	IN, PW	EP	INT, TRE
Wholesale trade. See Economic data					
Wilderness areas (5, 16)	AGR INT INT	FS LMB NPS	IN	EN	INT
Wildlife conservation (8, 16)	AGR COM INT MMC	FS NOAA FWS	AG, IN, MM	AG, EN, EP	COM, INT
Wiretapping (14)	JUS JUS	EOUS LIA	JU	JU	COM
Witness protection (14)	JUS	MS	JU	JU	COM

Women. See Abortion, Child
  support, Day care, Discrim-
  ination, Family planning,
  Prenatal care					

	Parent Agencies	Agency Subunits	House Committees	Senate Committees	Appropriations Subcommittees
Wood. See Timber resources					
Work hours. See Labor standards					
Workers compensation (6, 12)	LAB	WCP	ED	LA	LAB
Workplace hazards. See Occupational safety					
World fairs. See Expositions					
World health. See Epidemiology, Foreign aid, International organizations					
World peace. See International arbitration, International claims, International organizations					
Youth. See Child abuse, Juvenile delinquency, Missing children					

Part 2

General Subject Categories

SPECIFIC SUBJECT CATEGORIES BY GENERAL SUBJECT CATEGORY

AGRICULTURE (1)

Agricultural credit

Agricultural development

Agricultural markets

Agricultural production

Agricultural research

Agricultural subsidies

Agricultural surpluses

Commodity regulation

Crops

Dairy industry

Economic data

Fibers

Fruits

Grains

Herbicides

Horticulture

Insects

Irrigation

Land management

Livestock

Meat

Pesticides

Plants

Poultry

Rural areas

Soil conservation

Sugar

Tobacco industry

Weather

COMMERCE (2)

Advertising

Alcoholic beverages

Antitrust law

Automobile industry

Aviation industry

Billboards

Broadcasting

Bus lines

Business assistance

Business regulation

Commercial law

Commodity regulation

Consumer protection

Economic controls

Economic data

Energy consumption

Energy prices

Energy production

Exports

Expositions

Franchises

Freight

Gross National Product

Ground transportation

Harbors

Imports

Industrial technology

Inland waterways

Insurance industry

Interest rates

International communication

International trade

International transportation

Land sales

Lotteries

Maritime industry

COMMERCE (2)

Mineral leases

Mining industry

Moving industry

Multinatinal corporations

Negotiable instruments

Numismatics

Panama Canal

Passenger ships

Philately

Pipelines

Plastics

Postal Service

Precious metals

Precious stones

Product labeling

Product liability

Proprietary data

Railroad industry

Recording industry

Resource shortages

Rural areas

Securities industry

Small business

Space commercialization

Sports

Tariffs

Technology transfer

Telecommunications

Tourism

Trademarks

Trucking industry

Water transportation

COMMUNICATION (3)

Advertising

Arts

Billboards

Broadcasting

Charitable organizations

Computer technology

Copyrights

Federal records

Government information

Government publications

International communication

Journalistic confidentiality

Nonprofit organizations

Obscenity

Privacy

Proprietary data

Public broadcasting

Public demonstrations

Recording industry

Religious institutions

Space communication

Telecommunications

COMMUNITY DEVELOPMENT (4)

Agricultural development

Airports

Bridges

Business assistance

Credit programs

Dams

Depressed areas

Disaster relief

Harbors

Highway construction

Inland waterways

Insurance programs

Land sales

COMMUNITY DEVELOPMENT (4)

Military installations

Public buildings

Public housing

Real estate industry

Rural areas

Small business

Tunnels

Waste management

Water power

EDUCATION (5)

Adult education

Architecture

Arts

Bilingual education

Compensatory education

Consumer education

Crime prevention

Education data

Education research

Elementary education

Government fellowships

Higher education

Historic preservation

Home economics

Humanities

Juvenile delinquency

Learning disabilities

Libraries

Literacy

Monuments

Museums

Nonprofit organizations

Numismatics

Nutrition

Philately

Physical education

Preschool education

Preventive medicine

Private schools

Public broadcasting

Public schools

Rehabilitation services

Secondary education

Service academies

Social sciences

Sports

Student loans

Veterans

Vocational education

Volunteer services

Wilderness areas

EMPLOYMENT (6)

Aliens

Apprenticeship

Asbestos

Congressional employees

Day care

Drug testing

Economic data

Fringe benefits

Government employees

Labor relations

Labor standards

Marine safety

Migrant workers

Mine safety

Occupational safety

EMPLOYMENT (6)

Pensions

Polygraphs

Radiation

Retirement

Unemployment compensation

Unemployment rate

Veterans

Vocational education

Vocational rehabilitation

Wages

Workers compensation

ENERGY (7)

Coal

Electric power

Energy conservation

Energy consumption

Energy data

Energy prices

Energy production

Energy research

Energy storage

Hydroelectric power

Mineral leases

Natural gas

Nuclear energy

Nuclear facilities

Offshore drilling

Outer continental shelf

Petroleum

Pipelines

Public utilities

Resource shortages

Water power

ENVIRONMENTAL AFFAIRS (8)

Acid rain

Air pollution

Atmosphere

Coal

Earthquake research

Energy storage

Environmental protection

Environmental research

Flood control

Hazardous materials

Herbicides

Hydroelectric power

Industrial pollution

Marine resources

Mineral resources

Mining industry

Noise pollution

Nuclear facilities

Nuclear safety

Nuclear waste

Ocean use

Oceanography

Oil spills

Pesticides

Petroleum

Pipelines

Population growth

Public lands

Public utilities

Radiation

Radon

Recreation areas

Rights-of-way

Technology transfer

Territorial waters

ENVIRONMENTAL AFFAIRS (8)

Timber resources

Toxic substances

Waste management

Water pollution

Weather

Wildlife conservation

FINANCIAL AFFAIRS (9)

Accounting

Agricultural credit

Bank deposits

Bank regulation

Bankruptcy

Budget administration

Budget deficits

Budget formulation

Business investment

Consumer credit

Consumer Price Index

Credit programs

Credit unions

Currency

Customs

Debt collection

Debt management

Economic controls

Economic data

Financial institutions

Foreclosure

Foreign currency

Foreign taxes

Funding gaps

Government borrowing

Government securities

Government spending

Gross National Product

Health insurance

Housing industry

Impoundments

Individual retirement
  accounts

Interest rates

International finance

Local governments

Money supply

Mortgage loans

Multinational corporations

Negotiable instruments

Pensions

Precious metals

Public debt

Real estate industry

Revenue sharing

Securities industry

Social Security

State governments

Student loans

Tariffs

Taxation

Trust funds

Welfare

GOVERNMENTAL AFFAIRS (10)

Accounting

Administrative law

Advisory committees

Architecture

Budget administration

Budget deficits

Budget formulation

Capitol facilities

GOVERNMENTAL AFFAIRS (10)

Census

Citizenship

Civil-military relations

Congressional districts

Congressional employees

Congressional operations

Congressional organization

Congressional oversight

Congressional powers

Congressional-executive relations

Corrupt practices

Debt management

Diplomatic service

District of Columbia

Elections

Eminent domain

Executive branch operations

Executive branch organization

Executive privilege

Federal courts

Federal judges

Federal paperwork

Federal property

Federal records

Flag of the U.S.

Funding gaps

Government borrowing

Government contracts

Government corporations

Government employees

Government ethics

Government information

Government procurement

Government publications

Government securities

Government spending

Holidays

Identity papers

Impeachment

Impoundments

Inspectors General

Interagency relations

Intergovernmental relations

Interstate relations

Judicial administration

Lobbying

Local governments

Mapping

Members of Congress

Money supply

Naturalization

Pensions

Physical security

Political asylum

Postal Service

Presidency

Public administration

Public buildings

Public debt

Revenue sharing

Seal of the U.S.

Separation of powers

Space exploration

State boundaries

State governments

Taxation

Territories

Vice-Presidency

Voting

War powers

White House facilities

HEALTH (11)

Abortion

Acquired immune deficiency
  syndrome (AIDS)

Air pollution

Alcoholism

Allergies

Animals

Arthritis

Asbestos

Automobile industry

Aviation safety

Bacteriology

Blood

Building standards

Cancer

Chemicals

Child health

Communicable diseases

Construction industry

Consumer protection

Cosmetics industry

Dentistry

Drug abuse

Drug safety

Drug testing

Eating disroders

Environmental protection

Epidemiology

Explosives

Food inspection

Fruits

Handicapped

Hazardous materials

Health care

Health data

Health insurance

Health maintenance
  organizations

Heart disease

Herbicides

Highway safety

Hospital facilities

Hospital regulation

Immunization

Industrial pollution

Infant mortality

Marine safety

Meat

Medical devices

Medical research

Mental health

Mine safety

Mobile homes

Neurological diseases

Nuclear safety

Nursing homes

Nutrition

Occupational safety

Organ transplants

Pesticides

Physical education

Population growth

Prenatal care

Preventive medicine

Product labeling

Product safety

Radiation

Radon

Railroad safety

Rehabilitation services

Respiratory diseases

Skin diseases

Smoking

HEALTH (11)

Sugar

Toxic substances

Venereal disease

Veterans

Visual disorders

Water supply

INCOME SECURITY (12)

Aged

Agricultural credit

Agricultural subsidies

Child support

Crime victims

Crops

Disability benefits

Disaster relief

Food stamps

Fringe benefits

Handicapped

Homelessness

Housing management

Insurance programs

Pensions

Retirement

Social Security

Unemployment compensation

Welfare

Workers compensation

INTERNATIONAL AFFAIRS (13)

Agricultural markets

Agricultural surpluses

Airspace

Arms control

Arms exports

Border patrol

Citizens abroad

Customs

Diplomatic immunity

Diplomatic recognition

Diplomatic service

Disaster relief

Drug traffic

Espionage

Exports

Expositions

Extradition

Food distribution

Foreign agents

Foreign aid

Foreign currency

Foreign property

Foreign sovereign immunity

Foreign taxes

Foreign visitors

Human rights

Hunger

Immigration

Imports

Intelligence activities

International agreements

International arbitration

International boundaries

International claims

International communication

International crime

International finance

International law

International organizations

International trade

International transportation

INTERNATIONAL AFFAIRS (13)

International travel

International waters

Maritime industry

Military assistance

Military law

Multinational corporations

National security

Neutrality law

Nuclear proliferation

Ocean use

Panama Canal

Polar regions

Political asylum

Population growth

Refugees

Repatriation

Resource shortages

Tariffs

Technology transfer

Terrorism

Treason

Treaties

Volunteer services

War powers

Warfare

LEGAL AFFAIRS (14)

Abortion

Administrative law

Alcoholic beverages

Aliens

Antitrust law

Arson

Bankruptcy

Border patrol

Capital punishment

Citizenship

Civil disorders

Civil procedure

Civil rights

Commercial law

Computer security

Congressional powers

Congressional-executive
  relations

Constitutional amendments

Consumer credit

Copyrights

Correctional facilities

Corrupt practices

Counterfeiting

Crime data

Crime victims

Criminal procedure

Deportation

Diplomatic immunity

Discrimination

Drug traffic

Eminent domain

Espionage

Executive privilege

Expatriation

Explosives

Extradition

Federal charters

Federal courts

Federal judges

Firearms

Foreclosure

Foreign agents

Foreign sovereign immunity

LEGAL AFFAIRS (14)

Gambling

Government ethics

Government liability

Government litigation

Hijacking

Identity papers

Immigration

Impeachment

International claims

International crime

International law

Interstate relations

Journalistic confidentiality

Judicial administration

Judicial ethics

Judicial remedies

Juries

Juvenile delinquency

Law enforcement

Legal services

Lobbying

Naturalization

Neutrality law

Obscenity

Organized crime

Pardons

Parole

Patents

Polygraphs

Pornography

Prisoners

Privacy

Public demonstrations

Recording industry

Refugees

Seal of the U.S.

Sentences

Separation of powers

Smuggling

Subversive activities

Terrorism

Tobacco industry

Trademarks

Treason

Treaties

Trials

Violent crime

Voting

War powers

White collar crime

Wiretapping

Witness protection

NATIONAL DEFENSE (15)

Airspace

Armed forces

Arms control

Arms exports

Civil defense

Government contracts

Intelligence activities

International agreements

International waters

Marine Corps

Military assistance

Military installations

Military law

Military operations

Military personnel

Military research

National Guard

NATIONAL DEFENSE (15)

National security

Nuclear proliferation

Nuclear testing

Panama Canal

Selective Service

Service academies

Space communication

Strategic stockpiles

Subversive activities

Territorial waters

Terrorism

Treaties

Warfare

Weapons

NATURAL RESOURCES (16)

Acid rain

Air pollution

Animals

Birds

Coal

Coastal zone management

Dams

Endangered species

Fire control

Flood control

Forestry

Geology

Grazing lands

Historic preservation

Indians

Inland waterways

Insects

Irrigation

Land management

Mapping

Marine resources

Maritime industry

Mineral leases

Mineral resources

Natural gas

Nuclear energy

Ocean use

Oceanography

Outer continental shelf

Petroleum

Plants

Precious metals

Precious stones

Public lands

Recreation areas

Resource shortages

Soil conservation

Strategic stockpiles

Timber resources

Undersea exploration

Water pollution

Water supply

Wilderness areas

Wildlife conservation

SCIENCE & TECHNOLOGY (17)

Aeronautics

Agricultural research

Air pollution

Astronomy

Atmosphere

Aviation safety

Biotechnology

Building standards

Chemicals

SCIENCE & TECHNOLOGY (17)

Coastal zone management

Computer security

Computer technology

Drug safety

Drug testing

Earthquake research

Electric power

Electrical standards

Energy conservation

Energy production

Energy research

Environmental research

Explosives

Fire control

Genetics

Geology

Ground transportation

Highway safety

Industrial technology

Laboratory research

Marine resources

Medical devices

Medical research

Military research

Noise pollution

Nuclear energy

Nuclear testing

Nuclear waste

Oceanography

Offshore drilling

Organ transplants

Patents

Pipelines

Plastics

Polar regions

Privacy

Product safety

Radiation

Railroad safety

Recording industry

Soil conservation

Space commercialization

Space communication

Space exploration

Technological risk

Technology transfer

Telecommunications

Undersea exploration

Waste management

Water pollution

Water supply

Water transportation

Weapons

Weather

Weights and measures

SOCIAL SERVICES (18)

Aged

Agricultural surpluses

Charitable organizations

Child abuse

Child health

Child nutrition

Child support

Day care

Disability benefits

Family planning

Family services

Food distribution

Handicapped

Homelessness

SOCIAL SERVICES (18)

Hospital regulation

Hunger

Indians

Learning disabilities

Migrant workers

Missing children

Nursing homes

Prenatal care

Refugees

Rehabilitation services

Religious institutions

Retirement

Social Security

Trust funds

Vocational rehabilitation

Welfare

TRANSPORTATION (19)

Aeronautics

Airports

Automobile industry

Aviation industry

Bridges

Bus lines

Freight

Ground transportation

Harbors

Highway construction

Highway safety

Hijacking

Inland waterways

Marine safety

Mass transit

Mobile homes

Moving industry

Ocean use

Oil spills

Passenger ships

Railroad industry

Railroad safety

Rights-of-way

Time zones

Trucking industry

Tunnels

Water transportation

URBAN AFFAIRS (20)

Building standards

Construction industry

Credit programs

Depressed areas

District of Columbia

Homelessness

Homesteading

Housing industry

Housing management

Insurance programs

Intergovernmental relations

Land sales

Local governments

Mass transit

Mortgage loans

Public housing

Real estate industry

Slum clearance

Small business

Waste management

PARENT AGENCIES AND COMMITTEES BY GENERAL SUBJECT CATEGORY

	Parent Agencies	House Committees	Senate Committees	Appropriations Subcommittees
AGRICULTURE (1)	AGR CFTC FCA	AG (JEC)	AG	AGR INT
COMMERCE (2)	CFTC COM CPSC ENER EXIM FCC FMC FRB FTC ICC IDCA ITC JUS PCC SBA SEC STA TRA TRE	AG BA EN FA IN JU MM SB SC WM (JEC)	AG BA CO EN EP FI FR JU SB	AGR COM ENER FA TRA TRE VA
COMMUNICATION (3)	COM EDU EOP FCC FTC IBB JUS NARA NFAH PS USIA	ED EN FA GO JU PO SC	CO FR GA JU LA	COM INT LAB TRE
COMMUNITY DEVELOPMENT (4)	AGR COM DEF FEMA SBA TRA TVA	AG AR EN PW SB	AG AR CO EP SB	AGR COM MC TRA VA
EDUCATION (5)	ACTION CPSC EDU FAC GPO LC NCLIS NFAH NSF SI USIP VA	AGI ED HA IN VA	AGI LA RU VA	INT LAB LEG VA

	Parent Agencies	House Committees	Senate Committees	Appropriations Subcommittees
EMPLOYMENT (6)	EEOC	AGI	AGI	LAB
	FLRA	ED	GA	TRE
	FMCS	GO	LA	
	FMSH	PO	VA	
	LAB	VA		
	NLRB	(JEC)		
	NMB			
	OPM			
	OSHR			
	PBGC			
	VA			
ENERGY (7)	DEF	AR	AR	DEF
	ENER	EN	EN	ENER
	INT	IN	EP	INT
	NRC	PW		
	TVA	SC (JEC)		
ENVIRONMENTAL AFFAIRS (8)	COM	EN	CO	COM
	ENER	IN	EN	ENER
	EOP	MM	EP	INT
	EPA	PW		TRA
	FEMA	SC		VA
	INT			
	MMC			
	TRA			
FINANCIAL AFFAIRS (9)	AGR	AG	AG	AGR
	CBO	BA	BA	COM
	COM	BU	BU	FA
	EOP	EN	CO	LEG
	FCA	FA	FI	TRE
	PDIC	GO	FR	VA
	FHLBB	VA	GA	
	FRB	WM	VA	
	FSLIC	(JEC)		
	FTC			
	GAO			
	GNMA			
	HUD			
	IDCA			
	NCUA			
	PBGC			
	SEC			
	TRE			
	VA			
GOVERNMENTAL AFFAIRS (10)	ACIR	BA	BA	COM
	ACUS	BU	BU	INT
	ARC	DC	EP	LEG
	CBO	FA	ET	TRE
	COM	GO	FI	
	EOP	HA	FR	
	FAC	IN	GA	
	FEC	JU	JU	
	FLRA	PO	RU	
	FRB	RU		
	GAO	ST		
	GPO	WM		
	GSA	(JCP)		

	Parent Agencies	House Committees	Senate Committees	Appropriations Subcommittees
GOVERNMENTAL AFFAIRS (10)	JUS LC MSPB NARA NCPC OPM PADC PRC PS SCO STA TRE			
HEALTH (11)	AGR CPSC EPA FMSH HHS LAB NRC NTSB OSHR TRA VA	AG AGI ED EN IN VA WM	AG AGI CO EP FI LA VA	AGR ENER LAB TRA VA
INCOME SECURITY (12)	AGR FEMA HHS HUD LAB PBGC VA	AG AGI BA ED GO VA WM (JEC)	AG AGI BA FI LA VA	AGR LAB VA
INTERNATIONAL AFFAIRS (13)	ACDA AGR COM DEF EOP EXIM FCC FMC FRB IBB IDCA ITC PCC PCO SCEC STA TRA TRE USIA USIP	AG AR BA EN FA INT MM WM	AG AR BA CO FI FR INT	AGR COM DEF FA TRA TRE
LEGAL AFFAIRS (14)	ACUS CRC CRT EEOC FCC FEC FTC JUS LSC STA TRE	EN FA GO HA JU	CO FR GA JU RU	COM LEG TRE

	Parent Agencies	House Committees	Senate Committees	Appropriations Subcommittees
NATIONAL DEFENSE (15)	ACDA DEF ENER EOP FEMA PCC SSS STA	AR EN FA INT	AR EN FR INT	COM DEF ENER MC
NATURAL RESOURCES (16)	AGR COM DEF ENER EPA INT MMC TVA	AG AR EN IN PW	AG AR EN EP IN	AGR COM ENER INT VA
SCIENCE & TECHNOLOGY (17)	AGR COM DEF ENER EOP HHS INT NASA NSF OTA SI	AG AR ED EN IN PW SC	AG AR CO EN EP LA	AGR COM DEF ENER INT LAB VA
SOCIAL SERVICES (18)	ACTION AGR EDU HHS HUD LAB VA	AG AGI BA ED EN VA WM	AG AGI BA FI IN LA VA	AGR LAB VA
TRANSPORTATION (19)	FMC ICC NASA NTSB TRA	EN MM PW SC	CO EP	COM TRA VA
URBAN AFFAIRS (20)	GNMA HUD NCPC PADC SBA TRA	BA DC IN PW SB	BA EP GA SB	DC INT VA

Part 3

Parent Agencies

SPECIFIC SUBJECT CATEGORIES BY PARENT AGENCY

ACTION

Volunteer services

Administrative Conference
of the United States

Administrative law

Public administration

Advisory Commission on
Intergovernmental Relations

Intergovernmental relations

Local governments

State governments

Agriculture Department

Agricultural credit

Agricultural development

Agricultural markets

Agricultural production

Agricultural research

Agricultural subsidies

Agricultural surpluses

Animals

Birds

Child nutrition

Consumer education

Crops

Dairy industry

Disaster relief

Economic data

Endangered species

Environmental protection

Exports

Fibers

Fire control

Flood control

Food distribution

Food inspection

Food stamps

Foreclosure

Foreign aid

Forestry

Fruits

Grains

Herbicides

Home economics

Horticulture

Hunger

Insects

International trade

Irrigation

Land management

Livestock

Meat

Nutrition

Pesticides

Plants

Poultry

Public lands

Recreation areas

Rural areas

Soil conservation

Sugar

Timber resources

Tobacco industry

Water supply

Wilderness areas

Wildlife conservation

Architect of the Capitol

Capitol facilities

Arms Control and
Disarmament Agency

Arms control

Arms exports

Nuclear proliferation

Nuclear testing

Civil Rights Commission

Civil rights

Voting

Commerce Department

Air pollution

Atmosphere

Biotechnology

Broadcasting

Building standards

Business assistance

Business investment

Census

Chemicals

Coastal zone management

Computer security

Computer technology

Congressional districts

Customs

Depressed areas

Economic data

Electrical standards

Endangered species

Energy conservation

Environmental protection

Environmental research

Exports

Expositions

Fire control

Flood control

Food inspection

Franchises

Government publications

Gross National Product

Harbors

Imports

Industrial technology

International finance

International trade

International travel

Laboratory research

Local governments

Mapping

Marine resources

Mineral leases

Multinational corporations

Neutrality law

Ocean use

Oceanography

Offshore drilling

Patents

Plastics

Population growth

Precious stones

Product safety

Public broadcasting

Radiation

Resource shortages

Revenue sharing

Small business

Space commercialization

State governments

Commerce Department

Strategic stockpiles

Tariffs

Technology transfer

Telecommunications

Territorial waters

Tourism

Trademarks

Undersea exploration

Water pollution

Weather

Weights and measures

Wildlife conservation

Commodity Futures
Trading Commission

Commodity regulation

Precious metals

Sugar

Congressional Budget Office

Budget deficits

Budget formulation

Credit programs

Economic data

Government spending

Health insurance

Pensions

Public debt

Social Security

Taxation

Trust funds

Consumer Product
Safety Commission

Consumer education

Consumer protection

Explosives

Hazardous materials

Plastics

Product labeling

Product liability

Product safety

Toxic substances

Copyright Royalty Tribunal

Copyrights

Recording industry

Defense Department

Airspace

Armed forces

Arms control

Arms exports

Astronomy

Civil defense

Coastal zone management

Dams

Drug testing

Drug traffic

Exports

Flood control

Government contracts

Government information

Government procurement

Inland waterways

Intelligence activities

International waters

Mapping

Marine Corps

Military assistance

Military installations

Military law

Defense Department

Military operations
Military personnel
Military research
National Guard
National security
Nuclear proliferation
Nuclear testing
Ocean use
Oceanography
Polygraphs
Privacy
Service academies
Space communication
Strategic stockpiles
Technology transfer
Telecommunications
Undersea exploration
Wages
Warfare
Weapons
White collar crime

Education Department

Adult education
Bilingual education
Compensatory education
Discrimination
Education data
Education research
Elementary education
Handicapped
Higher education
Home economics
Homelessness
Indians

Juvenile delinquency
Learning disabilities
Libraries
Literacy
Migrant workers
Preschool education
Private schools
Public schools
Rehabilitation services
Secondary education
Sports
Student loans
Veterans
Vocational education
Vocational rehabilitation

Energy Department

Arms control
Coal
Electric power
Energy conservation
Energy consumption
Energy data
Energy prices
Energy production
Energy research
Energy storage
Environmental research
Exports
Hydroelectric power
National security
Natural gas
Nuclear energy
Nuclear facilities
Nuclear proliferation
Nuclear safety

Energy Department

Nuclear testing

Nuclear waste

Offshore drilling

Petroleum

Pipelines

Proprietary data

Public utilities

Radiation

Resource shortages

Strategic stockpiles

Weapons

Environmental Protection Agency

Acid rain

Air pollution

Asbestos

Atmosphere

Automobile industry

Chemicals

Energy storage

Environmental protection

Environmental research

Hazardous materials

Herbicides

Industrial pollution

Mining industry

Noise pollution

Oil spills

Pesticides

Radiation

Radon

Technology transfer

Toxic substances

Waste management

Water pollution

Equal Employment Opportunity Commission

Apprenticeship

Discrimination

Vocational rehabilitation

Executive Office of the President

Accounting

Acid rain

Aeronautics

Arms control

Biotechnology

Budget administration

Budget deficits

Budget formulation

Civil-military relations

Computer security

Computer technology

Congressional-executive
 relations

Credit programs

Customs

Debt collection

Drug testing

Drug traffic

Economic controls

Economic data

Energy production

Energy research

Environmental research

Espionage

Executive branch operations

Executive branch
 organization

Executive privilege

Exports

Federal paperwork

Federal Election Commission

Elections

Presidency

Vice-Presidency

Federal Emergency Management Agency

Arson

Business assistance

Civil defense

Civil disorders

Crime victims

Disaster relief

Fire control

Homelessness

Insurance programs

Nuclear safety

Small business

Strategic stockpiles

Federal Home Loan Bank Board

Bank regulation

Consumer credit

Financial institutions

Mortgage loans

Federal Labor Relations Authority

Government employees

Labor relations

Federal Maritime Commission

Freight

Harbors

International trade

International transportation

Maritime industry

Passenger ships

Water transportation

Federal Mediation and Conciliation Service

Labor relations

Federal Mine Safety and Health Review Commission

Mine safety

Federal Reserve System

Bank regulation

Consumer credit

Credit unions

Currency

Economic data

Financial institutions

Foreign currency

Government securities

Insurance industry

Interest rates

International finance

Money supply

Negotiable instruments

Precious metals

Securities industry

Federal Savings and Loan Insurance Corporation

Bank deposits

Financial institutions

Federal Trade Commission

Advertising

Antitrust law

Automobile industry

Federal Trade Commission

Business regulation

Commercial law

Consumer credit

Consumer education

Consumer protection

Debt collection

Franchises

Insurance industry

Land sales

Lotteries

Product labeling

Product safety

Proprietary data

Sports

Fine Arts Commission

Architecture

Monuments

Public buildings

General Accounting Office

Accounting

Budget administration

Congressional operations

Congressional oversight

Congressional-executive relations

Credit programs

Debt collection

Debt management

Executive branch operations

Government contracts

Government corporations

Government liability

Government spending

Impoundments

Inspectors General

Interagency relations

Intergovernmental relations

Public administration

General Services Administration

Advisory committees

Architecture

Computer security

Computer technology

Consumer education

Executive branch operations

Federal property

Government information

Government procurement

Physical security

Public administration

Public buildings

Small business

Strategic stockpiles

White House facilities

Government National Mortgage Association

Mortgage loans

Government Printing Office

Computer technology

Government publications

Libraries

Health and Human Services Department

Abortion

Acquired immune deficiency
  syndrome (AIDS)

Advertising

Health and Human Services Department

Aged

Alcoholism

Allergies

Animals

Arthritis

Bacteriology

Biotechnology

Blood

Cancer

Child abuse

Child health

Child support

Communicable diseases

Consumer education

Cosmetics industry

Day care

Dentistry

Disability benefits

Discrimination

Drug abuse

Drug safety

Drug testing

Eating disorders

Environmental research

Epidemiology

Family planning

Family services

Food inspection

Genetics

Handicapped

Health care

Health data

Health insurance

Health maintenance organizations

Heart disease

Herbicides

Homelessness

Hospital facilities

Hospital regulation

Immunization

Indians

Infant mortality

Juvenile delinquency

Learning disabilities

Medical devices

Medical research

Mental health

Migrant workers

Missing children

Neurological diseases

Nursing homes

Nutrition

Occupational safety

Organ transplants

Pesticides

Physical education

Population growth

Prenatal care

Preschool education

Preventive medicine

Product labeling

Product safety

Radiation

Refugees

Rehabilitation services

Respiratory diseases

Retirement

Skin diseases

Smoking

Social Security

<u>Health and Human Services</u>
<u>Department</u>

Student loans

Sugar

Toxic substances

Venereal disease

Visual disorders

Welfare

<u>Housing and Urban</u>
<u>Development Department</u>

Building standards

Construction industry

Depressed areas

Discrimination

Energy conservation

Environmental research

Foreclosure

Homelessness

Homesteading

Housing industry

Housing management

Indians

Insurance programs

Land management

Land sales

Mobile homes

Mortgage loans

Nursing homes

Public housing

Real estate industry

Slum clearance

Waste management

<u>Interior Department</u>

Animals

Architecture

Birds

Coal

Dams

Earthquake research

Endangered species

Energy production

Energy research

Environmental protection

Flood control

Forestry

Geology

Grazing lands

Historic preservation

Hydroelectric power

Indians

Irrigation

Land management

Mapping

Marine resources

Mine safety

Mineral leases

Mineral resources

Mining industry

Monuments

Natural gas

Offshore drilling

Outer continental shelf

Petroleum

Physical security

Precious metals

Precious stones

Public demonstrations

Public lands

Recreation areas

Resource shortages

Rights-of-way

Interior Department

State boundaries

Territories

Timber resources

Water power

Water supply

White House facilities

Wilderness areas

Wildlife conservation

International Broadcasting
Board

International communication

International Development
Cooperation Agency

Disaster relief

Foreign aid

International finance

International trade

Population growth

International Trade Commission

Customs

Exports

Imports

International trade

Precious stones

Tariffs

Interstate Commerce Commission

Antitrust law

Bus lines

Business regulation

Commercial law

Freight

Ground transportation

Inland waterways

Moving industry

Railroad industry

Trucking industry

Water transportation

Justice Department

Aliens

Antitrust law

Bankruptcy

Border patrol

Capital punishment

Citizenship

Civil disorders

Civil procedure

Civil rights

Commercial law

Computer security

Congressional employees

Congressional power

Congressional-executive
  relations

Constitutional amendments

Correctional facilities

Corrupt practices

Crime data

Crime prevention

Crime victims

Criminal procedure

Debt collection

Deportation

Diplomatic immunity

Drug traffic

Elections

Eminent domain

Environmental protection

Justice Department

Espionage

Executive privilege

Expatriation

Extradition

Federal charters

Federal courts

Federal judges

Foreign agents

Foreign visitors

Gambling

Government information

Government liability

Government litigation

Hijacking

Identity papers

Immigration

Impeachment

Indians

Intelligence activities

International crime

Interstate relations

Journalistic confidentiality

Judicial administration

Judicial ethics

Judicial remedies

Juries

Juvenile delinquency

Law enforcement

Lobbying

Lotteries

Members of Congress

Missing children

Naturalization

Neutrality law

Obscenity

Organized crime

Pardons

Parole

Political asylum

Polygraphs

Pornography

Presidency

Prisoners

Privacy

Product liability

Proprietary data

Public demonstrations

Refugees

Religious institutions

Sentences

Separation of powers

Smuggling

State boundaries

Subversive activities

Territorial waters

Terrorism

Treason

Treaties

Trials

Vice-Presidency

Violent crime

Voting

War powers

White collar crime

Wiretapping

Witness protection

Labor Department

Aliens

Apprenticeship

Asbestos

Labor Department

Chemicals

Construction industry

Consumer Price Index

Day care

Discrimination

Drug testing

Economic data

Explosives

Fringe benefits

Government contracts

Hazardous materials

Labor relations

Labor standards

Marine safety

Migrant workers

Mine safety

Occupational safety

Pensions

Polygraphs

Radiation

Retirement

Toxic substances

Unemployment compensation

Unemployment rate

Veterans

Vocational rehabilitation

Wages

Welfare

Workers compensation

Legal Services Corporation

Legal services

Library of Congress

Civil-military relations

Congressional operations

Congressional organization

Congressional oversight

Congressional power

Congressional-executive
  relations

Copyrights

Federal records

Libraries

Separation of powers

War powers

Marine Mammal Commission

Wildlife conservation

Merit Systems Protection
Board

Government employees

National Aeronautics and
Space Administration

Aeronautics

Astronomy

Atmosphere

Space commercialization

Space communication

Space exploration

National Archives and
Records Administration

Federal records

Privacy

Public administration

National Capital
Planning Commission

District of Columbia

Historic preservation

Monuments

Public buildings

National Commission on Libraries
and Information Science

Libraries

National Credit Union
Administration

Consumer credit

Credit unions

Financial institutions

National Foundation on
the Arts and Humanities

Architecture

Arts

Government fellowhips

Humanities

Museums

Nonprofit organizations

Public broadcasting

Public buildings

National Labor Relations Board

Labor relations

National Mediation Board

Labor relations

National Science Foundation

Astronomy

Atmosphere

Biotechnology

Chemicals

Computer technology

Earthquake research

Electrical standards

Energy research

Environmental research

Geology

Government fellowhips

Industrial technology

Laboratory research

Oceanography

Offshore drilling

Plastics

Polar regions

Social sciences

Technological risk

Undersea exploration

Weather

National Transportation
Safety Board

Aviation safety

Hazardous materials

Highway safety

Marine safety

Mass transit

Pipelines

Railroad safety

Nuclear Regulatory Commission

Nuclear facilities

Nuclear safety

Nuclear waste

Public utilities

Radiation

Occupational Safety and
Health Review Commission
Occupational safety

Office of Personnel Management

Drug testing

Fringe benefits

Government employees

Government ethics

Health insurance

Holidays

Labor relations

Pensions

Polygraphs

Public administration

Retirement

Veterans

Wages

Office of Technology Assessment

Biotechnology

Chemicals

Computer technology

Drug safety

Drug testing

Energy production

Energy research

Environmental research

Genetics

Health care

Industrial pollution

Industrial technology

Laboratory research

Marine resources

Military research

Mineral resources

National security

Nuclear energy

Nuclear waste

Oceanography

Polygraphs

Privacy

Radiation

Space exploration

Strategic stockpiles

Technological risk

Telecommunications

Undersea exploration

Waste management

Weapons

Weather

Panama Canal Commission
Panama Canal

Peace Corps
Volunteer services

Pennsylvania Avenue
Development Corporation

District of Columbia

Historic preservation

Pension Benefit Guaranty
Corporation
Pensions

Postal Rate Commission
Postal Service

Postal Service

Charitable organizations

Lotteries

Nonprofit organizations

Obscenity

Philately

Pornography

Postal Service

White collar crime

Securities and Exchange Commission

Accounting

Advertising

Bankruptcy

Business investment

Economic data

Financial institutions

International finance

Negotiable instruments

Securities industry

White collar crime

Security and Cooperation in Europe Commission

Human rights

Selective Service System

Selective Service

Small Business Administration

Business assistance

Business investment

Business regulation

Disaster relief

Economic data

Franchises

Government contracts

Industrial technology

Insurance programs

International trade

Rural areas

Small business

Veterans

Smithsonian Institution

Aeronautics

Animals

Arts

Geology

Government fellowships

Historic preservation

Horticulture

Humanities

Indians

Insects

Museums

Plants

Precious stones

Space exploration

Special Counsel's Office

Government employees

State Department

Airspace

Arms control

Arms exports

Citizens abroad

Citizenship

Copyrights

Diplomatic immunity

Diplomatic recognition

State Department
Diplomatic service
Drug traffic
Environmental research
Expatriation
Exports
Extradition
Foreign aid
Foreign sovereign immunity
Foreign visitors
Human rights
Immigration
Imports
Intelligence activities
International agreements
International arbitration
International boundaries
International communication
International crime
International finance
International law
International organizations
International trade
International transportation
International travel
International waters
Marine resources
Maritime industry
Military assistance
Military law
Multinational corporations
National security
Neutrality law
Nuclear proliferation
Ocean use
Panama Canal

Patents
Polar regions
Political asylum
Population growth
Refugees
Repatriation
Seal of the U.S.
Strategic stockpiles
Technology transfer
Territories
Terrorism
Trademarks
Treaties
Undersea exploration
Warfare

Tennessee Valley Authority
Electric power
Flood control
Forestry
Irrigation
Public utilities
Recreation areas
Water power
Water supply

Transportation Department
Air pollution
Airports
Atmosphere
Automobile industry
Aviation industry
Aviation safety
Billboards
Bridges
Business assistance

Transportation Department
Civil defense
Drug traffic
Freight
Ground transportation
Harbors
Hazardous materials
Highway construction
Highway safety
Hijacking
Inland waterways
International trade
International transportation
International waters
Marine safety
Maritime industry
Mass transit
Mobile homes
Ocean use
Oil spills
Passenger ships
Pipelines
Railroad industry
Railroad safety
Rights-of-way
Service academies
Smuggling
Space commercialization
Territorial waters
Time zones
Tunnels
Water transportation

Treasury Department
Accounting
Advertising

Alcoholic beverages
Arson
Bank regulation
Border patrol
Budget administration
Budget deficits
Budget formulation
Business investment
Charitable organizations
Consumer credit
Counterfeiting
Credit programs
Currency
Customs
Day care
Debt collection
Debt management
Drug traffic
Eminent domain
Explosives
Federal paperwork
Financial institutions
Firearms
Foreign aid
Foreign currency
Foreign property
Foreign taxes
Fringe benefits
Funding gaps
Government borrowing
Government securities
Government spending
Identity papers
Imports
Individual retirement
  accounts

Treasury Department

Interest rates

International communication

International finance

International organizations

International trade

Law enforcement

Lobbying

Local governments

Money supply

Multinational corporations

Neutrality law

Nonprofit organizations

Numismatics

Philately

Physical security

Precious metals

Presidency

Product labeling

Public debt

Real estate industry

Religious institutions

Resource shortages

Retirement

Revenue sharing

Securities industry

Smuggling

State governments

Tariffs

Taxation

Technology transfer

Tobacco industry

Trust funds

Vice-Presidency

White collar crime

United States Information Agency

Expositions

Foreign visitors

International communication

International travel

United States Institute of Peace

International arbitration

Veterans Affairs Department

Disability benefits

Health care

Hospital regulation

Insurance programs

Mortgage loans

Pensions

Rehabilitation services

Veterans

Vocational education

Vocational rehabilitation

CONGRESSIONAL COMMITTEES BY PARENT AGENCY

	House Committees	Senate Committees	Appropriations Subcommittees
ACTION (5)	ED	LA	LAB
Administrative Conference of the United States (10, 14)	GO, JU	GA, JU	TRE
Advisory Commission on Inter-governmental Relations (10)	GO	GA	TRE
Agriculture Department (1, 4, 9, 11, 12, 13, 16, 17, 18)	AG (JEC)	AG	AGR, INT
Architect of the Capitol (10)	HA	RU	LEG
Arms Control and Disarmament Agency (13, 15)	FA	FR	COM
Civil Rights Commission (14)	JU	JU	COM
Commerce Department (2, 3, 4, 8, 9, 10, 13, 16, 17)	EN, MM, SC (JEC)	CO, EP	COM
Commodity Futures Trading Commission (1, 2)	AG	AG	AGR
Congressional Budget Office (9, 10)	BU	BU	LEG
Consumer Product Safety Commission (2, 5, 11)	EN	CO	VA
Copyright Royalty Tribunal (14)	JU	JU	LEG
Defense Department (4, 7, 13, 15, 16, 17)	AR, INT	AR, INT	DEF, MC
Education Department (3, 5, 18)	ED	LA	LAB
Energy Department (2, 7, 8, 15, 16, 17)	EN, IN, SC (JEC)	EN	ENER, INT
Environmental Protection Agency (8, 11, 16)	EN	EP	VA
Equal Employment Opportunity Commission (6, 14)	ED	LA	COM
Executive Office of the President (8, 9, 10, 13, 14, 15, 17)	AR, BA, EN, GO, JU, SC (JEC)	AR, BA, CO, EP, GA, JU	COM, DEF, TRE, VA
Export-Import Bank of the United States (2, 13)	BA (JEC)	BA	FA
Farm Credit Administration (1, 9)	AG	AG	AGR
Federal Communications Commission (2, 3, 13, 14)	EN	CO	COM
Federal Deposit Insurance Corporation (9)	BA	BA	*

*This is a self-sustaining agency and does not receive any appropriated funds

	House Committees	Senate Committees	Appropriations Subcommittees
Federal Election Commission (10, 14)	HA	RU	TRE
Federal Emergency Management Agency (4, 8, 12, 15)	GO	GA	VA
Federal Home Loan Bank Board (9)	BA	BA	VA
Federal Labor Relations Authority (6, 10)	ED, PO	GA, LA	TRE
Federal Maritime Commission (2, 13, 19)	MM	CO	COM
Federal Mediation and Conciliation Service (6)	ED	LA	LAB
Federal Mine Safety and Health Review Commission (6, 11)	ED	LA	LAB
Federal Reserve System (2, 9, 10, 13)	BA (JEC)	BA	*
Federal Savings and Loan Insurance Corporation (9)	BA	BA	VA
Federal Trade Commission (2, 3, 9, 14)	EN	CO	COM
Fine Arts Commission (5, 10)	ED	LA	INT
General Accounting Office (9, 10)	GO	GA	LEG
General Services Administration (10)	GO	GA	TRE
Government National Mortgage Association (9, 20)	BA	BA	VA
Government Printing Office (5, 10)	HA (JCP)	RU	LEG
Health and Human Services Department (11, 12, 17, 18)	AGI, ED, EN, WM	AGI, FI, LA	AGR, LAB
Housing and Urban Development Department (9, 12, 18, 20)	BA (JEC)	BA	VA
Interior Department (7, 8, 16, 17)	IN	EN, EP, IN	ENER, INT
International Broadcasting Board (3, 13)	FA	FR	COM
International Development Cooperation Agency (2, 9, 13)	FA	FR	FA
International Trade Commission (2, 13)	WM (JEC)	FI	COM
Interstate Commerce Commission (2, 19)	EN	CO	TRA

*This is a self-sustaining agency and does not receive any appropriated funds

	House Committees		Senate Committees	Appropriations Subcommittees
Justice Department (2, 3, 10, 14)	JU		JU	COM
Labor Department (6, 11, 12, 18)	ED	(JEC)	LA	LAB
Legal Services Corporation (14)	JU		LA	COM
Library of Congress (5, 10)	HA		RU	LEG
Marine Mammal Commission (8, 16)	MM		EP	COM
Merit Systems Protection Board (10)	PO		GA	TRE
National Aeronautics and Space Administration (17, 19)	SC		CO	VA
National Archives and Records Administration (3, 10)	GO		GA	TRE
National Capital Planning Commission (10, 20)	DC		GA	INT
National Commission on Libraries and Information Science (5)	ED		LA	LAB
National Credit Union Administration (9)	BA		BA	VA
National Foundation on the Arts and Humanities (3, 5)	ED		LA	INT
National Labor Relations Board (6)	ED		LA	LAB
National Mediation Board (6)	ED		LA	LAB
National Science Foundation (5, 17)	SC		CO	VA
National Transportation Safety Board (11, 19)	PW		CO	TRA
Nuclear Regulatory Commission (7, 11)	IN		EP	ENER
Occupational Safety and Health Review Commission (6, 11)	ED		LA	LAB
Office of Personnel Management (6, 10)	GO, PO		GA	TRE
Office of Technology Assessment (17)	SC		CO	LEG
Panama Canal Commission (2, 13, 15)	AR, MM		AR, CO	TRA
Peace Corps (13)	FA		FR	FA
Pennsylvania Avenue Development Corporation (10, 20)	IN		EP	INT
Pension Benefit Guaranty Corporation (6, 9, 12)	ED		LA	LAB

	House Committees	Senate Committees	Appropriations Subcommittees
Postal Rate Commission (10)	PO	GA	TRE
Postal Service (3, 10)	PO	GA	TRE
Securities and Exchange Commission (2, 9)	BA, EN (JEC)	BA	COM
Security and Cooperation in Europe Commission (13)	FA	FR	COM
Selective Service System (15)	AR	AR	VA
Small Business Administration (2, 4, 20)	SB (JEC)	SB	COM
Smithsonian Institution (5, 16, 17)	HA	RU	INT
Special Counsel's Office (10)	PO	GA	TRE
State Department (2, 10, 13, 14, 15)	FA	FR	COM, FA
Tennessee Valley Authority (4, 7, 16)	PW	EN, EP	ENER
Transportation Department (2, 4, 8, 11, 13, 19, 20)	EN, PW	CO, EP	COM, TRA
Treasury Department (2, 9, 10, 13, 14)	BA, EN, FA, GO, JU, WM (JEC)	BA, CO, FI, FR, GA, JU	TRE
United States Information Agency (3, 13)	FA	FR	COM
United States Insitute of Peace (5, 13)	ED	FR, LA	LAB
Veterans Affairs Department (5, 6, 9, 11, 12, 18)	VA	VA	VA

Part 4

Congressional Committees

SPECIFIC SUBJECT CATEGORIES BY CONGRESSIONAL COMMITTEE

HOUSE OF REPRESENTATIVES

Aging

Aged

Agriculture

Agricultural credit

Agricultural development

Agricultural markets

Agricultural production

Agricultural research

Agricultural subsidies

Agricultural surpluses

Animals

Birds

Child nutrition

Commodity regulation

Consumer education

Crops

Dairy industry

Disaster relief

Economic data

Exports

Fibers

Fire control

Flood control

Food distribution

Food inspection

Food stamps

Foreclosure

Forestry

Fruits

Grains

Grazing lands

Herbicides

Home economics

Horticulture

Hunger

Insects

International trade

Irrigation

Land management

Livestock

Meat

Nutrition

Pesticides

Plants

Poultry

Rural areas

Soil conservation

Sugar

Timber resources

Tobacco industry

Water supply

Wildlife conservation

Appropriations

Budget administration

Credit programs

District of Columbia

Executive branch operations

Funding gaps

Government spending

Impoundments

Armed Services

Airspace

Armed forces

Arms control

Arms exports

HOUSE OF REPRESENTATIVES

Armed Services

Civil defense

Government contracts

Government procurement

Intelligence activities

Mapping

Marine Corps

Military assistance

Military installations

Military law

Military operations

Military personnel

Military research

National Guard

National security

Nuclear energy

Nuclear proliferation

Nuclear testing

Selective Service

Service academies

Space communication

Strategic stockpiles

Telecommunications

Wages

Warfare

Weapons

Banking, Finance, and
Urban Affairs

Advertising

Bank deposits

Bank regulation

Building standards

Business assistance

Business investment

Commercial law

Construction industry

Consumer credit

Credit programs

Credit unions

Crime victims

Currency

Depressed areas

Discrimination

Economic controls

Economic data

Exports

Financial institutions

Foreclosure

Foreign currency

Government contracts

Government securities

Gross National Product

Historic preservation

Homelessness

Homesteading

Housing industry

Housing management

Individual retirement
accounts

Insurance industry

Insurance programs

Interest rates

International finance

International organizations

International trade

Land management

Land sales

Money supply

Mortgage loans

HOUSE OF REPRESENTATIVES

Banking, Finance, and
Urban Affairs

Negotiable instruments

Numismatics

Nursing homes

Precious metals

Public housing

Real estate industry

Securities industry

Slum clearance

White collar crime

Budget

Budget deficits

Budget formulation

Credit programs

Economic data

Government spending

Public debt

Social Security

Taxation

Trust funds

District of Columbia

District of Columbia

Education and Labor

Adult education

Aged

Aliens

Apprenticeship

Architecture

Arts

Asbestos

Bilingual education

Chemicals

Child abuse

Child nutrition

Child support

Compensatory education

Construction industry

Consumer Price Index

Day care

Debt collection

Disability benefits

Discrimination

Economic data

Education data

Education research

Elementary education

Explosives

Family services

Food distribution

Fringe benefits

Government contracts

Government fellowships

Handicapped

Higher education

Home economics

Homelessness

Humanities

Hunger

Juvenile delinquency

Labor relations

Labor standards

Learning disabilities

Libraries

Literacy

Migrant workers

Mine safety

HOUSE OF REPRESENTATIVES

Education and Labor

Missing children

Museums

Nutrition

Occupational safety

Pensions

Polygraphs

Preschool education

Private schools

Public schools

Radiation

Refugees

Rehabilitation services

Retirement

Secondary education

Sports

Student loans

Unemployment rate

Vocational education

Vocational rehabilitation

Volunteer services

Wages

Welfare

Workers compensation

Energy and Commerce

Accounting

Acid rain

Acquired immune deficiency
  syndrome (AIDS)

Advertising

Aged

Air pollution

Alcoholic beverages

Alcoholism

Allergies

Antitrust law

Arthritis

Asbestos

Atmosphere

Automobile industry

Aviation industry

Bacteriology

Blood

Broadcasting

Bus lines

Business investment

Business regulation

Cancer

Chemicals

Child health

Coal

Commercial law

Communicable diseases

Consumer credit

Consumer education

Consumer protection

Cosmetics industry

Debt collection

Dentistry

Discrimination

Drug abuse

Drug safety

Drug testing

Eating disorders

Electric power

Energy conservation

Energy consumption

Energy data

Energy prices

HOUSE OF REPRESENTATIVES

Energy and Commerce

Energy production

Energy research

Energy storage

Environmental protection

Epidemiology

Exports

Expositions

Family planning

Food inspection

Franchises

Genetics

Government publications

Ground transportation

Handicapped

Hazardous materials

Health care

Health data

Health insurance

Health maintenance organizations

Heart disease

Herbicides

Highway safety

Homelessness

Hospital facilities

Hospital regulation

Hydroelectric power

Immunization

Imports

Industrial pollution

Industrial technology

Infant mortality

Inland waterways

Insurance industry

International communication

International trade

International transportation

International travel

Interstate relations

Learning disabilities

Mapping

Medical devices

Medical research

Mental health

Mining industry

Mobile homes

Moving industry

Natural gas

Negotiable instruments

Neurological diseases

Noise pollution

Nuclear energy

Nuclear facilities

Nuclear safety

Nuclear waste

Nursing homes

Nutrition

Offshore drilling

Oil spills

Organ transplants

Pesticides

Petroleum

Physical education

Pipelines

Plastics

Population growth

Precious stones

Prenatal care

Preventive medicine

Product labeling

HOUSE OF REPRESENTATIVES

Energy and Commerce

Product liability

Product safety

Proprietary data

Public broadcasting

Public utilities

Radiation

Radon

Railroad industry

Railroad safety

Recording industry

Rehabilitation services

Resource shortages

Respiratory diseases

Securities industry

Skin diseases

Smoking

Space communication

Sports

Technology transfer

Telecommunications

Time zones

Tobacco industry

Tourism

Toxic substances

Trucking industry

Venereal disease

Visual disorders

Vocational rehabilitation

Waste management

Water pollution

Water power

Water supply

Water transportation

Foreign Affairs

Airspace

Arms control

Arms exports

Border patrol

Citizens abroad

Civil-military relations

Congressional-executive relations

Customs

Diplomatic immunity

Diplomatic recognition

Diplomatic service

Disaster relief

Drug traffic

Espionage

Expatriation

Exports

Expositions

Extradition

Foreign aid

Foreign property

Foreign visitors

Human rights

Hunger

Imports

Intelligence activities

International agreements

International arbitration

International boundaries

International claims

International communication

International crime

International finance

International law

HOUSE OF REPRESENTATIVES

Foreign Affairs

International organizations

International trade

International transportation

International travel

International waters

Military assistance

Military law

Multinational corporations

National security

Neutrality law

Nuclear proliferation

Nuclear testing

Ocean use

Polar regions

Political asylum

Population growth

Refugees

Repatriation

Smuggling

Terrorism

Treaties

Volunteer services

War powers

Warfare

Government Operations

Accounting

Administrative law

Advisory committees

Architecture

Budget administration

Budget formulation

Computer security

Computer technology

Congressional operations

Congressional organization

Congressional oversight

Congressional-executive
  relations

Consumer education

Drug testing

Eminent domain

Executive branch operations

Executive branch organization

Executive privilege

Federal paperwork

Federal property

Federal records

Government contracts

Government corporations

Government ethics

Government information

Government procurement

Government spending

Homelessness

Identity papers

Inspectors General

Interagency relations

Intergovernmental relations

Labor relations

Local governments

Philately

Physical security

Postal Service

Presidency

Privacy

Public administration

Revenue sharing

Separation of powers

HOUSE OF REPRESENTATIVES

Government Operations

State governments

Vice-Presidency

House Administration

Arts

Capitol facilities

Congressional employees

Congressional operations

Elections

Federal records

Government publications

Historic preservation

Humanities

Libraries

Lobbying

Members of Congress

Monuments

Museums

Physical security

Presidency

Vice-Presidency

Intelligence

Intelligence activities

Interior and Insular Affairs

Birds

Coal

Coastal zone management

Dams

District of Columbia

Earthquake research

Electric power

Endangered species

Energy production

Environmental protection

Environmental research

Flood control

Forestry

Geology

Grazing lands

Historic preservation

Hydroelectric power

Indians

Inland waterways

Irrigation

Land management

Mapping

Marine resources

Mineral leases

Mineral resources

Mining industry

Monuments

Nuclear energy

Nuclear facilities

Nuclear safety

Nuclear waste

Offshore drilling

Outer continental shelf

Petroleum

Pipelines

Public lands

Public utilities

Radiation

Recreation areas

Resource shortages

Rights-of-way

Territories

Timber resources

HOUSE OF REPRESENTATIVES

Interior and Insular Affairs

Water power

Water supply

White House facilities

Wilderness areas

Wildlife conservation

Judiciary

Abortion

Administrative law

Alcoholic beverages

Aliens

Antitrust law

Arson

Bankruptcy

Border patrol

Capital punishment

Citizenship

Civil disorders

Civil procedure

Civil rights

Civil-military relations

Commercial law

Computer security

Congressional districts

Congressional power

Congressional-executive relations

Constitutional amendments

Copyrights

Correctional facilities

Corrupt practices

Counterfeiting

Crime data

Crime prevention

Crime victims

Criminal procedure

Deportation

Diplomatic immunity

Discrimination

Drug traffic

Elections

Espionage

Executive privilege

Expatriation

Explosives

Extradition

Federal charters

Federal courts

Federal judges

Firearms

Flag of the U.S.

Foreign agents

Foreign sovereign immunity

Foreign visitors

Gambling

Government ethics

Government information

Government liability

Government litigation

Hijacking

Holidays

Immigration

Impeachment

International crime

Interstate relations

Journalistic confidentiality

Judicial administration

Judicial ethics

Judicial remedies

Juries

HOUSE OF REPRESENTATIVES

Judiciary

Juvenile delinquency

Law enforcement

Legal services

Lobbying

Lotteries

Missing children

Naturalization

Obscenity

Organized crime

Pardons

Parole

Patents

Political asylum

Polygraphs

Pornography

Presidency

Prisoners

Privacy

Product liability

Public demonstrations

Recording industry

Refugees

Religious institutions

Seal of the U.S.

Sentences

Separation of powers

Smuggling

State boundaries

Subversive activities

Terrorism

Trademarks

Treason

Trials

Vice-Presidency

Violent crime

Voting

White collar crime

Wiretapping

Witness protection

Merchant Marine and Fisheries

Animals

Coastal zone management

Endangered species

Environmental research

Freight

Harbors

International trade

International transportation

International waters

Marine resources

Marine safety

Maritime industry

Mineral leases

Ocean use

Oceanography

Offshore drilling

Oil spills

Outer continental shelf

Panama Canal

Passenger ships

Service academies

Territorial waters

Undersea exploration

Water pollution

Water transportation

Weather

Wildlife conservation

HOUSE OF REPRESENTATIVES

Post Office and Civil Service

Census

Charitable organizations

Drug testing

Federal paperwork

Fringe benefits

Government employees

Government ethics

Government procurement

Health insurance

Health maintenance organizations

Holidays

Labor relations

Lotteries

Occupational safety

Pensions

Philately

Polygraphs

Postal Service

Public administration

Retirement

Wages

Public Works and Transportation

Airports

Automobile industry

Aviation industry

Aviation safety

Billboards

Bridges

Business assistance

Capitol facilities

Dams

Depressed areas

Disaster relief

District of Columbia

Electric power

Eminent domain

Flood control

Freight

Ground transportation

Harbors

Hazardous materials

Highway construction

Highway safety

Inland waterways

International transportation

Mass transit

Mobile homes

Oil spills

Pipelines

Public buildings

Public utilities

Trucking industry

Tunnels

Waste management

Water pollution

Water power

Water supply

Water transportation

White House facilities

Rules

Budget formulation

Congressional-executive
  relations

Congressional operations

Congressional organization

Congressional oversight

Impoundments

HOUSE OF REPRESENTATIVES

Science, Space, and Technology

Aeronautics

Agricultural research

Air pollution

Astronomy

Atmosphere

Aviation industry

Biotechnology

Chemicals

Coal

Computer security

Computer technology

Earthquake research

Electric power

Electrical standards

Endangered species

Energy research

Environmental research

Explosives

Fire control

Genetics

Geology

Government publications

Ground transportation

Handicapped

Herbicides

Highway safety

Industrial technology

Laboratory research

Marine resources

Medical research

Mineral resources

Natural gas

Noise pollution

Nuclear energy

Nuclear waste

Nutrition

Ocean use

Oceanography

Patents

Petroleum

Plastics

Polar regions

Privacy

Radiation

Social sciences

Space commercialization

Space communication

Space exploration

Strategic stockpiles

Technological risk

Technology transfer

Telecommunications

Toxic substances

Waste management

Water pollution

Water supply

Weather

Weights and measures

Small Business

Antitrust law

Business assistance

Business investment

Business regulation

Commercial law

Disaster relief

Exports

Franchises

Government contracts

HOUSE OF REPRESENTATIVES

Small Business

Industrial technology

Insurance programs

International trade

Occupational safety

Rural areas

Small business

Standards of Official Conduct

Corrupt practices

Members of Congress

Veterans Affairs

Disability benefits

Health care

Hospital regulation

Insurance programs

Mortgage loans

Pensions

Rehabilitation services

Veterans

Vocational education

Vocational rehabilitation

Ways and Means

Accounting

Aged

Budget administration

Budget deficits

Business investment

Charitable organizations

Customs

Day care

Debt collection

Debt management

Federal paperwork

Foreign taxes

Fringe benefits

Funding gaps

Government borrowing

Government securities

Handicapped

Health insurance

Health maintenance
   organizations

Homelessness

Imports

Individual retirement accounts

Interest rates

International finance

International trade

Lobbying

Multinational corporations

Nonprofit organizations

Nursing homes

Precious stones

Public debt

Real estate industry

Religious institutions

Retirement

Revenue sharing

Social Security

Tariffs

Taxation

Tobacco industry

Trust funds

Unemployment compensation

Welfare

SENATE

Aging

Jurisdiction is identical to
House Aging Committee

Agriculture, Nutrition, and Forestry

Jurisdiction is identical to
House Agriculture Committee

Appropriations

Jurisdiction is identical to
House Appropriations Committee

Armed Services

Jurisdiction is identical to
House Armed Services Committee
with the following exception:
includes Panama Canal

Banking, Housing, and Urban Affairs

Jurisdiction is identical to
House Banking, Finance, and
Urban Affairs Committee with
the following exceptions:
includes Accounting and Mass
transit; excludes Historic
preservation

Budget

Jurisdiction is identical to
House Budget Committee

Commerce, Science, and Transportation

Advertising

Aeronautics

Airports

Alcoholic beverages

Antitrust law

Astronomy

Atmosphere

Automobile industry

Aviation industry

Aviation safety

Biotechnology

Broadcasting

Bus lines

Business investment

Business regulation

Chemicals

Coastal zone management

Commercial law

Computer technology

Consumer credit

Consumer education

Consumer protection

Cosmetics industry

Debt collection

Discrimination

Drug testing

Earthquake research

Electrical standards

Endangered species

Environmental research

Explosives

Exports

Expositions

Fire control

Franchises

Freight

Genetics

Geology

Government publications

Ground transportation

Harbors

Hazardous materials

Herbicides

Highway safety

Imports

Industrial technology

Inland waterways

International communication

International trade

SENATE

Commerce, Science, and Transportation

International transportation

International travel

International waters

Interstate relations

Laboratory research

Mapping

Marine resources

Marine safety

Maritime industry

Mobile homes

Moving industry

Natural gas

Noise pollution

Ocean use

Oceanography

Offshore drilling

Oil spills

Outer continental shelf

Panama Canal

Passenger ships

Patents

Pipelines

Plastics

Polar regions

Precious stones

Privacy

Product labeling

Product liability

Product safety

Proprietary data

Public broadcasting

Radiation

Railroad industry

Railroad safety

Recording industry

Resource shortages

Service academies

Space commercialization

Space communication

Space exploration

Sports

Technological risk

Technology transfer

Telecommunications

Territorial waters

Time zones

Tobacco industry

Tourism

Trucking industry

Undersea exploration

Water pollution

Water transportation

Weather

Weights and measures

Energy and Natural Resources

Coal

Coastal zone management

Dams

Electric power

Energy conservation

Energy consumption

Energy data

Energy prices

Energy production

Energy research

Energy storage

Environmental protection

SENATE

Energy and Natural Resources

Flood control

Forestry

Geology

Grazing lands

Harbors

Historic preservation

Hydroelectric power

Industrial pollution

Inland waterways

Irrigation

Land management

Mineral leases

Mineral resources

Mining industry

Monuments

Natural gas

Nuclear energy

Nuclear safety

Nuclear waste

Offshore drilling

Outer continental shelf

Petroleum

Pipelines

Public lands

Public utilities

Recreation areas

Resource shortages

Rights-of-way

Territories

Timber resources

Undersea exploration

Water power

Water supply

Wilderness areas

Wildlife conservation

Environment and Public Works

Acid rain

Air pollution

Animals

Asbestos

Atmosphere

Automobile industry

Aviation industry

Billboards

Birds

Bridges

Business assistance

Capitol facilities

Coal

Dams

Depressed areas

Disaster relief

District of Columbia

Earthquake research

Electric power

Eminent domain

Endangered species

Environmental protection

Environmental research

Flood control

Ground transportation

Harbors

Hazardous materials

Herbicides

Highway construction

Highway safety

Industrial pollution

Inland waterways

SENATE

Environment and Public Works

International transportation

Mapping

Marine resources

Noise pollution

Nuclear energy

Nuclear facilities

Nuclear safety

Nuclear waste

Ocean use

Oil spills

Public buildings

Public utilities

Radiation

Radon

Respiratory diseases

Toxic substances

Tunnels

Waste management

Water pollution

Water power

Water supply

Water transportation

White House facilities

Wildlife conservation

Ethics

Jurisdiction is identical to
House Standards of Official
Conduct Committee

Finance

Jurisdiction is identical to
House Ways and Means Committee

Foreign Relations

Jurisdiction is identical to
House Foreign Affairs Committee with the following exception: includes Foreign agents

Governmental Affairs

Jurisdiction is identical to
House Government Operations
Committee with the following
exceptions: includes

Arson

Census

Charitable organizations

Debt collection

District of Columbia

Fringe benefits

Government employees

Health insurance

Health maintenance
   organizations

Lobbying

Lotteries

Nuclear energy

Nuclear facilities

Nuclear proliferation

Nuclear waste

Occupational safety

Organized crime

Pensions

Polygraphs

Public buildings

Retirement

Wages

SENATE

Indian Affairs

Indians

Intelligence

Jursidiction is identical to
House Intelligence Committee

Judiciary

Jurisdiction is identical to
House Judiciary Committee with
the following exceptions:
includes Insurance industry;
excludes Foreign agents,
Legal services, and Lobbying

Labor and Human Resources

Acquired immune deficiency
  syndrome (AIDS)

Adult education

Aged

Alcoholism

Aliens

Allergies

Apprenticeship

Architecture

Arthritis

Arts

Asbestos

Bacteriology

Bilingual education

Biotechnology

Blood

Cancer

Chemicals

Child abuse

Child health

Child support

Communicable diseases

Compensatory education

Construction industry

Consumer Price Index

Cosmetics industry

Day care

Dentistry

Disability benefits

Discrimination

Drug abuse

Drug safety

Drug testing

Eating disorders

Economic data

Education data

Education research

Elementary education

Epidemiology

Explosives

Family planning

Family services

Food inspection

Genetics

Government contracts

Government fellowships

Health care

Health data

Health insurance

Health maintenance
  organizations

Heart disease

Higher education

Home economics

Homelessness

Hospital facilities

Hospital regulation

Humanities

Hunger

SENATE

Labor and Human Resources

Immunization

Infant mortality

Juvenile delinquency

Labor relations

Labor standards

Learning disabilities

Legal services

Libraries

Literacy

Medical devices

Medical research

Mental health

Migrant workers

Mine safety

Missing children

Museums

Neurological diseases

Nursing homes

Nutrition

Occupational safety

Organ transplants

Pensions

Pesticides

Physical education

Polygraphs

Population growth

Prenatal care

Preschool education

Preventive medicine

Private schools

Public schools

Radiation

Refugees

Rehabilitation services

Respiratory diseases

Retirement

Secondary education

Skin diseases

Smoking

Social sciences

Sports

Student loans

Toxic substances

Unemployment rate

Venereal disease

Visual disorders

Vocational education

Vocational rehabilitation

Volunteer services

Wages

Welfare

Workers compensation

Rules and Administration

Jurisdiction is identical to House Administration Committee with the following exceptions: includes Congressional organization and Impoundments

Small Business

Jurisdiction is identical to House Small Business Committee

Veterans Affairs

Jurisdiction is identical to House Veterans Affairs Committee

JOINT PANELS

Joint Committee on Printing

Government publications

Joint Economic Committee

Business regulation

Commercial law

Consumer Price Index

Economic data

Gross National Product

Housing industry

Industrial technology

Interest rates

International trade

Labor relations

Multinational corporations

Public debt

Small business

Tariffs

Taxation

Unemployment rate

Wages

PARENT AGENCIES AND APPROPRIATIONS SUBCOMMITTEES
BY LEGISLATIVE COMMITTEE

House Committees	Parent Agencies	Senate Committees		Appropriations Subcommittees
Aging (5, 6, 11, 12, 18)	EDU HHS HUD LAB	AGI		LAB VA
Agriculture (1, 4, 9, 11, 12, 13, 16, 17, 18)	AGR CFTC FCA	AG	(JEC)	AGR
Armed Services (4, 7, 13, 15, 16, 17)	DEF EOP PCC SSS	AR		DEF MC
Banking, Finance, and Urban Affairs (2, 9, 10, 12, 13, 18, 20)	EOP EXIM FDIC FHLBB FRB FSLIC GNMA HUD NCUA SEC TRE	BA (JEC)		COM TRE VA
Budget (9, 10)	CBO	BU		LEG
District of Columbia (10, 20)	NCPC	GA		DC
Education and Labor (3, 5, 6, 11, 12, 17, 18)	ACTION EDU EEOC FAC FLRA FMCS FMSH HHS LAB NCLIS NFAH NLRB NMB OSHR PBGC USIP	LA (JEC)		INT LAB
Energy and Commerce (2, 3, 4, 7, 8, 9, 11, 13, 14, 15, 16, 17, 18, 19)	COM CPSC ENER EOP EPA FCC FTC HHS ICC SEC TRA TRE	BA CO EN EP LA (JEC)		COM ENER INT LAB TRA TRE VA

House Committees	Parent Agencies	Senate Committees	Appropriations Subcommittees
Foreign Affairs (2, 3, 9, 10, 13, 14, 15)	ACDA IBB IDCA PCO SCEC STA TRE USIA	FR	COM FA
Government Operations (3, 6, 9, 10, 12, 14)	ACIR ACUS EOP FEMA GAO GSA NARA TRE	GA	LEG TRE VA
House Administration (5, 10, 14)	ARC GPO LC SI	RU (JCP)	INT LEG
Intelligence (13, 15)	DEF EOP JUS STA TRE	INT	DEF
Interior and Insular Affairs (2, 5, 7, 8, 10, 11, 16, 17, 20)	INT NRC PADC	EN EP IN	ENER INT
Judiciary (2, 3, 10, 14)	ACUS CRC CRT JUS LSC TRE	JU	COM TRE
Merchant Marine and Fisheries (2, 8, 13, 19)	COM FMC MMC PCC	CO (JEC)	COM TRA
Post Office and Civil Service (3, 6, 10)	FLRA MSPB OPM PRC PS SCO	GA	TRE
Public Works and Transportation (4, 7, 8, 16, 17, 19, 20)	NTSB TRA TVA	CO EP GA	TRA TRE
Rules (10)		RU	LEG
Science, Space, and Technology (2, 3, 7, 8, 17, 20)	COM ENER EOP NASA NSF OTA	CO EN	COM ENER INT VA
Small Business (2, 4, 20)	SBA	SB (JEC)	COM

House Committees	Parent Agencies	Senate Committees	Appropriations Subcommittees
Standards of Official Conduct (10)	JUS	ET	LEG
Veterans Affairs (5, 6, 9, 11, 12, 18)	VA	VA	VA
Ways and Means (2, 9, 10, 11, 12, 13, 18)	HHS ITC TRE	FI (JEC)	COM LAB TRE

Senate Committees	House Committees
Aging (Identical to House Aging Committee)	

Agriculture, Nutrition, and Forestry (Identical to House Agriculture Committee)

Armed Services (Identical to House Armed Services Committee)

Banking, Housing, and Urban Affairs (Identical to House Banking, Finance, and Urban Affairs Committee)

Budget (Identical to House Budget Committee)

Senate Committees	Parent Agencies	House Committees	Appropriations Subcommittees
Commerce, Science, and Transportation (2, 3, 4, 8, 9, 11, 13, 14, 17, 19)	COM CPSC EOP FCC FMC FTC ICC NASA NSF NTSB OTA PCC TRA TRE	EN MM SC (JEC)	COM TRA TRE VA
Energy and Natural Resources (2, 7, 8, 15, 16, 17)	ENER INT TVA	EN IN SC (JEC)	ENER INT
Environment and Public Works (2, 4, 7, 8, 10, 11, 16, 17, 19, 20)	COM EPA INT MMC NRC PADC TRA TVA	EN MM SC	COM ENER INT TRA VA

Ethics (Identical to House Standards of Official Conduct Committee)

Finance (Identical to House Ways and Means Committee)

Foreign Relations (Identical to House Foreign Affairs Committee with addition of one Parent Agency: USIP)

Senate Committees	Parent Agencies	House Committees	Appropriations Subcommittees
Governmental Affairs (3, 6, 9, 10, 14, 20)	ACIR	DC	DC
	ACUS	GO	LEG
	EOP	PO	TRE
	FEMA		
	FLRA		
	GAO		
	GSA		
	MSPB		
	NARA		
	NCPC		
	OPM		
	PRC		
	PS		
	SCO		
Indian Affairs (16, 18)	EDU	IN	INT
	HHS		LAB
	HUD		
	LAB		

Intelligence (Identical to House Intelligence Committee)

Judiciary (Identical to House Judiciary Committee)

Senate Committees	Parent Agencies	House Committees	Appropriations Subcommittees
Labor and Human Resources (3, 5, 6, 11, 12, 17, 18)	ACTION	ED	COM
	EDU	EN	INT
	EEOC		LAB
	FAC	(JEC)	
	FLRA		
	FMCS		
	FMSH		
	HHS		
	LAB		
	LSC		
	NCLIS		
	NFAH		
	NLRB		
	NMB		
	OSHR		
	PBGC		
	USIP		

Rules and Administration (Identical to House Administration Committee)

Small Business (Identical to House Small Business Committee)

Veterans Affairs (Identical to House Veterans Affairs Committee)

Joint Committees	Parent Agencies	House Committees	Senate Committees	Appropriations Subcommittees
Economic (1, 2, 6, 7, 9, 12)	AGR	AG	AG	AGR
	COM	BA	BA	COM
	ENER	ED	CO	ENER
	EOP	EN	EN	FA
	EXIM	MM	FI	LAB
	FRB	SB	LA	TRE
	HUD	WM	SB	VA
	ITC			
	LAB			
	SBA			
	SEC			
	TRE			
Printing (10)	GPO	HA	RU	LEG

Part 5

Appropriations Subcommittees

SPECIFIC SUBJECT CATEGORIES BY APPROPRIATIONS SUBCOMMITTEE

Agriculture, Rural Development, and Related Agencies

Agricultural credit

Agricultural development

Agricultural markets

Agricultural production

Agricultural research

Agricultural subsidies

Agricultural surpluses

Animals

Birds

Child nutrition

Commodity regulation

Crops

Dairy industry

Disaster relief

Fibers

Flood control

Food distribution

Food inspection

Food stamps

Foreclosure

Fruits

Grains

Herbicides

Home economics

Horticulture

Hunger

Insects

Irrigation

Livestock

Meat

Nutrition

Pesticides

Plants

Poultry

Rural areas

Soil conservation

Sugar

Tobacco industry

Departments of Commerce, Justice, State, and the Judiciary and Related Agencies

Accounting

Administrative law

Advertising

Air pollution

Airspace

Aliens

Antitrust law

Arms control

Atmosphere

Automobile industry

Bankruptcy

Biotechnology

Border patrol

Broadcasting

Building standards

Business assistance

Business investment

Business regulation

Capital punishment

Census

Chemicals

Citizens abroad

Citizenship

Civil disorders

Civil procedure

Civil rights

<u>Departments</u> <u>of</u> <u>Commerce</u>,
<u>Justice</u>, <u>State</u>, <u>and the</u>
<u>Judiciary</u> <u>and</u> <u>Related</u>
<u>Agencies</u>

Coastal zone management

Commercial law

Computer security

Computer technology

Congressional districts

Constitutional amendments

Consumer credit

Consumer education

Consumer protection

Copyrights

Correctional facilities

Corrupt practices

Crime data

Crime prevention

Crime victims

Criminal procedure

Customs

Debt collection

Deportation

Depressed areas

Diplomatic immunity

Diplomatic recognition

Diplomatic service

Discrimination

Drug traffic

Economic data

Electrical standards

Eminent domain

Endangered species

Environmental research

Espionage

Executive privilege

Expatriation

Exports

Expositions

Extradition

Federal charters

Federal courts

Federal judges

Fire control

Firearms

Foreign agents

Foreign aid

Foreign sovereign immunity

Foreign visitors

Franchises

Freight

Gambling

Government corporations

Government information

Government liability

Government litigation

Gross National Product

Harbors

Hijacking

Human rights

Identity papers

Immigration

Impeachment

Imports

Industrial technology

Inland waterways

Insurance industry

International agreements

International boundaries

International claims

International communication

International crime

International finance

International law

Departments of Commerce, Justice, State, and the Judiciary and Related Agencies

International trade

International transportation

International travel

International waters

Interstate relations

Journalistic confidentiality

Judicial administration

Judicial ethics

Judicial remedies

Juries

Juvenile delinquency

Laboratory research

Law enforcement

Legal services

Lobbying

Local governments

Lotteries

Mapping

Marine resources

Maritime industry

Mineral leases

Multinational corporations

National security

Naturalization

Negotiable instruments

Neutrality law

Nuclear proliferation

Obscenity

Ocean use

Oceanography

Organized crime

Panama Canal

Pardons

Parole

Passenger ships

Patents

Plastics

Polar regions

Political asylum

Polygraphs

Pornography

Precious stones

Presidency

Prisoners

Privacy

Product labeling

Product liability

Product safety

Proprietary data

Public broadcasting

Public demonstrations

Recording industry

Refugees

Religious institutions

Repatriation

Resource shortages

Seal of the U.S.

Securities industry

Sentences

Separation of powers

Small business

Smuggling

Space communication

Sports

State boundaries

Strategic stockpiles

Subversive activities

Tariffs

Technology transfer

Departments of Commerce,
Justice, State, and the
Judiciary and Related
Agencies

Telecommunications

Territorial waters

Territories

Terrorism

Tourism

Trademarks

Treason

Treaties

Trials

Undersea exploration

Vice-Presidency

Violent crime

Voting

War powers

Warfare

Water pollution

Water transportation

Weather

Weights and measures

White collar crime

Wildlife conservation

Wiretapping

Witness protection

Defense Department

Armed forces

Arms control

Arms exports

Civil defense

Espionage

Government contracts

Government procurement

Intelligence activities

Mapping

Marine Corps

Military assistance

Military law

Military operations

Military personnel

Military research

National Guard

National security

Nuclear proliferation

Nuclear testing

Ocean use

Oceanography

Service academies

Strategic stockpiles

Technology transfer

Warfare

Weapons

District of Columbia

District of Columbia

Energy and Water Development

Coal

Dams

Electric power

Energy conservation

Energy consumption

Energy prices

Energy production

Energy research

Energy storage

Flood control

Hydroelectric power

Irrigation

Nuclear energy

Energy and Water Development

Nuclear facilities

Nuclear safety

Nuclear testing

Nuclear waste

Offshore drilling

Petroleum

Pipelines

Proprietary data

Public utilities

Radiation

Resource shortages

Water power

Water supply

Weapons

Foreign Assistance and
Related Programs

Arms exports

Exports

Foreign aid

Human rights

International finance

International organizations

International trade

Military assistance

Population growth

Volunteer services

Interior Department and
Related Agencies

Animals

Architecture

Arts

Birds

Coal

Earthquake research

Endangered species

Energy consumption

Energy data

Energy prices

Energy production

Energy research

Environmental protection

Fire control

Forestry

Geology

Grazing lands

Historic preservation

Humanities

Indians

Land management

Mapping

Marine resources

Mine safety

Mineral leases

Mineral resources

Mining industry

Monuments

Museums

Natural gas

Offshore drilling

Outer continental shelf

Petroleum

Precious metals

Precious stones

Public buildings

Public demonstrations

Public lands

Recreation areas

Rights-of-way

Territories

Timber resources

Interior Department and
Related Agencies

Water supply

White House facilities

Wilderness areas

Wildlife conservation

Departments of Labor, Health
and Human Services, and
Education, and Related
Agencies

Abortion

Acquired immune deficiency
  syndrome (AIDS)

Adult education

Aged

Alcoholism

Aliens

Allergies

Apprenticeship

Arthritis

Asbestos

Bacteriology

Bilingual education

Biotechnology

Blood

Cancer

Child abuse

Child health

Child support

Communicable diseases

Compensatory education

Consumer Price Index

Day care

Dentistry

Disability benefits

Discrimination

Drug abuse

Drug testing

Eating disorders

Economic data

Education data

Education research

Elementary education

Epidemiology

Family planning

Family services

Fringe benefits

Genetics

Government contracts

Government fellowships

Handicapped

Health care

Health data

Health insurance

Health maintenance
  organizations

Heart disease

Higher education

Home economics

Homelessness

Hospital facilities

Hospital regulation

Immunization

Indians

Infant mortality

Juvenile delinquency

Labor relations

Labor standards

Learning disabilities

Libraries

Literacy

Medical devices

Medical research

Departments of Labor, Health and Human Services, and Education, and Related Agencies

Mental health

Migrant workers

Mine safety

Missing children

Neurological diseases

Nursing homes

Occupational safety

Organ transplants

Pensions

Physical education

Polygraphs

Population growth

Prenatal care

Preschool education

Preventive medicine

Private schools

Public schools

Radiation

Refugees

Rehabilitation services

Respiratory diseases

Retirement

Secondary education

Skin diseases

Smoking

Social Security

Sports

Student loans

Toxic substances

Unemployment compensation

Unemployment rate

Venereal disease

Veterans

Visual disorders

Vocational education

Vocational rehabilitation

Volunteer services

Wages

Welfare

Workers compensation

Legislative Branch

Capitol facilities

Congressional employees

Congressional operations

Congressional organization

Congressional oversight

Congressional power

Congressional-executive relations

Constitutional amendments

Copyrights

Elections

Government publications

Impeachment

Libraries

Members of Congress

Separation of powers

War powers

Military Construction

Military installations

Transportation Department and Related Agencies

Airports

Automobile industry

Aviation industry

Aviation safety

Billboards

Transportation Department and Related Agencies

Bridges

Bus lines

Business assistance

Freight

Ground transportation

Harbors

Hazardous materials

Highway construction

Highway safety

Hijacking

Inland waterways

International transportation

Marine safety

Maritime industry

Mass transit

Moving industry

Oil spills

Panama Canal

Passenger ships

Pipelines

Railroad industry

Railroad safety

Rights-of-way

Service academies

Smuggling

Space commercialization

Territorial waters

Time zones

Trucking industry

Tunnels

Water transportation

Treasury, Postal Service and General Government

Accounting

Administrative law

Advisory committees

Alcoholic beverages

Arson

Bank regulation

Border patrol

Budget administration

Budget deficits

Budget formulation

Business investment

Charitable organizations

Civil-military relations

Computer security

Congressional-executive relations

Counterfeiting

Credit programs

Currency

Customs

Debt collection

Debt management

Drug testing

Drug traffic

Economic controls

Elections

Executive branch operations

Executive branch organization

Executive privilege

Explosives

Federal paperwork

Federal property

Federal records

Treasury, Postal Service
and General Government

Financial institutions

Firearms

Foreign currency

Foreign property

Foreign taxes

Fringe benefits

Funding gaps

Government borrowing

Government employees

Government ethics

Government information

Government procurement

Government securities

Government spending

Health insurance

Holidays

Identity papers

Impoundments

Individual retirement accounts

Inspectors General

Interagency relations

Interest rates

Intergovernmental relations

Labor relations

Law enforcement

Lobbying

Local governments

Money supply

Multinational corporations

Negotiable instruments

Nonprofit organizations

Numismatics

Pensions

Philately

Physical security

Polygraphs

Postal Service

Precious metals

Presidency

Privacy

Public administration

Public buildings

Public debt

Resource shortages

Retirement

Revenue sharing

Securities industry

State governments

Strategic stockpiles

Tariffs

Taxation

Tobacco industry

Trust funds

Vice-Presidency

Wages

White collar crime

White House facilities

Departments of Veterans
Affairs, Housing and Urban
Development, and Independent
Agencies

Acid rain

Aeronautics

Air pollution

Arson

Asbestos

Astronomy

Atmosphere

Bank deposits

Bank regulation

Departments of Veterans
Affairs, Housing and Urban
Development, and Independent
Agencies

Building standards

Chemicals

Civil defense

Computer technology

Construction industry

Consumer education

Consumer protection

Credit unions

Depressed areas

Disability benefits

Disaster relief

Electrical standards

Energy storage

Environmental protection

Environmental research

Financial institutions

Foreclosure

Government corporations

Hazardous materials

Health care

Herbicides

Homelessness

Homesteading

Hospital regulation

Housing industry

Housing management

Industrial pollution

Industrial technology

Insurance programs

Interest rates

Land sales

Mining industry

Mobile homes

Mortgage loans

Noise pollution

Oil spills

Pensions

Pesticides

Plastics

Polar regions

Product labeling

Product liability

Product safety

Public housing

Radiation

Radon

Real estate industry

Rehabilitation services

Selective Service

Slum clearance

Social sciences

Space commercialization

Space communication

Space exploration

Technological risk

Toxic substances

Undersea exploration

Veterans

Vocational education

Vocational rehabilitation

Waste management

Water pollution

Weather

PARENT AGENCIES AND LEGISLATIVE COMMITTEES
BY APPROPRIATIONS SUBCOMMITTEE

	Parent Agencies	House Committees	Senate Committees
Agriculture, Rural Development, and Related AGencies (1, 2, 4, 9, 11, 12, 16, 17, 18)	AGR (except FS) CFTC FCA FDA (HHS)	AG (JEC)	AG
Departments of Commerce, Justice, State, and the Judiciary and Related Agencies (2, 3, 4, 8, 9, 10, 13, 14, 15, 16, 17, 19)	ACDA COM CRC EEOC FCC FMC FTC IBB ITC JUS LSC MA (TRA) MMC SBA SCEC SEC STA (except INM, IOA, RPB) TRO (EOP) USIA	BA ED EN FA JU MM SB WM (JEC)	BA CO EP FI FR JU LA SB
Defense Department (7, 13, 15, 16, 17)	CIA (EOP) DEF	AR INT	AR INT
District of Columbia (10, 20)		DC	GA
Energy and Water Development (2, 7, 8, 11, 15, 16, 17)	ACE (DEF) ENER (except EIA, ERA, FEO) NRC RB (INT) TVA	EN IN PW (JEC)	EN EP
Foreign Assistance and Related Programs (2, 9, 13, 15)	EXIM IDCA INM (STA) IOA (STA) PCO RPB (STA)	AR FA	AR FR
Interior Department and Related Agencies (1, 3, 5, 7, 8, 10, 16, 17, 20)	EIA (ENER) ERA (ENER) FAC FEO (ENER) FS (AGR) INT (except RB) NCPC NFAH PADC SI	AG DC ED EN HA IN	AG EN EP GA IN LA RU

	Parent Agencies	House Committees	Senate Committees
Departments of Labor, Health and Human Services, and Education, and Related Agencies (3, 5, 6, 11, 12, 17, 18)	ACTION EDU FMCS FMSH HHS (except FDA) LAB NCLIS NLRB NMB OSHR PBGC USIP	AGI ED EN WM (JEC)	AGI FI LA
Legislative Branch (5, 9, 10, 14)	ARC CBO CRT GAO GPO LC OTA	BU GO HA JU RU ST (JCP)	BU ET GA JU RU
Military Construction (4, 15)	DEF	AR	AR
Transportation Department and Related Agencies (2, 4, 8, 11, 13, 19)	ICC NTSB PCC TRA (except MA)	EN MM PW	CO
Treasury, Postal Service and General Government (2, 3, 6, 9, 10, 13, 14)	ACIR ACUS EOP (except CEQ, CIA, STP, TRO) FEC FLRA GSA MSPB NARA OPM PRC PS SCO TRE	GO HA JU PO WM (JEC)	FI GA JU RU
Departments of Veterans Affairs, Housing and Urban Development, and Independent Agencies (2, 4, 5, 8, 9, 11, 12, 16, 17, 18, 19, 20)	CEQ (EOP) CPSC EPA FEMA FHLBB FSLIC GNMA HUD NASA NCUA NSF SSS STP (EOP) VA	BA EN GO SC VA (JEC)	BA CO EP GA VA

Index
(Agency/Committee Abbreviations)

Parent Agencies

ACDA   Arms Control and Disarmament Agency, 7, 36, 70, 71, 76, 94, 122, 137

ACIR   Advisory Commission on Intergovernmental Relations, 28, 31, 45, 69, 75, 94, 122, 124, 138

ACTION   49, 68, 71, 75, 94, 121, 124, 138

ACUS   Administrative Conference of the United States, 5, 40, 69, 70, 75, 94, 122, 124, 138

AGR   Agriculture Department, 6, 9, 11, 13, 14, 15, 16, 17, 18, 19, 20, 21, 22, 23, 24, 25, 26, 28, 29, 30, 31, 32, 36, 37, 38, 39, 41, 42, 43, 45, 46, 47, 50, 68, 69, 70, 71, 75, 94, 121, 124, 137

ARC   Architect of the Capitol, 10, 69, 76, 94, 122, 138

CBO   Congressional Budget Office, 9, 10, 14, 17, 24, 25, 37, 40, 46, 48, 69, 77, 94, 121, 138

CFTC   Commodity Futures Trading Commission, 12, 39, 46, 68, 77, 94, 121, 137

COM   Commerce Department, 6, 8, 9, 10, 11, 12, 13, 15, 16, 17, 18, 19, 20, 21, 22, 24, 25, 27, 29, 30, 31, 32, 33, 34, 35, 36, 37, 38, 39, 40, 41, 42, 43, 44, 45, 46, 47, 48, 49, 50, 68, 69, 70, 71, 76, 94, 121, 122, 123, 124, 137

CPSC   Consumer Product Safety Commission, 13, 20, 25, 38, 40, 47, 68, 70, 77, 94, 121, 123, 138

CRC   Civil Rights Commission, 11, 49, 70, 76, 94, 122, 137

CRT   Copyright Royalty Tribunal, 14, 41, 70, 77, 94, 122, 138

DEF   Defense Department, 6, 7, 8, 11, 12, 15, 17, 20, 21, 23, 24, 28, 29, 31, 32, 33, 34, 35, 36, 38, 39, 44, 45, 46, 48, 49, 50, 68, 69, 70, 71, 77, 94, 121, 122, 137, 138

EDU   Education Department, 5, 8, 12, 16, 18, 24, 25, 26, 27, 30, 31, 33, 39, 40, 41, 42, 44, 45, 46, 48, 49, 68, 71, 78, 94, 121, 124, 138

EEOC   Equal Employment Opportunity Commission, 7, 16, 49, 69, 70, 79, 94, 121, 124, 137

ENER   Energy Department, 7, 12, 18, 19, 20, 27, 35, 36, 37, 38, 40, 41, 42, 46, 50, 68, 69, 71, 78, 94, 121, 122, 123, 124, 137

EOP   Executive Office of the President, 5, 7, 9, 10, 11, 12, 13, 14, 15, 17, 18, 19, 20, 21, 23, 24, 27, 28, 29, 31, 32, 33, 34, 35, 36, 39, 40, 41, 45, 46, 47, 48, 49, 50, 68, 69, 70, 71, 79, 94, 121, 122, 123, 124, 137, 138

EPA   Environmental Protection Agency, 5, 6, 7, 8, 11, 19, 25, 27, 33, 35, 36, 37, 41, 46, 47, 49, 69, 70, 71, 79, 94, 121, 123, 138

EXIM   Export-Import Bank of the United States, 10, 20, 29, 68, 70, 80, 94, 121, 124, 137

FAC   Fine Arts Commission, 7, 34, 40, 68, 69, 82, 95, 121, 124, 137

FCA   Farm Credit Administration, 6, 68, 69, 80, 94, 121, 137

FCC   Federal Communications Commission, 5, 7, 9, 10, 29, 31, 36, 40, 41, 45, 46, 68, 70, 94, 121, 123, 137

Agency Subunits

AA   Aging Administration (HHS), 5

ACE   Army Corps of Engineers (DEF), 12, 15, 21, 28

ACS   Agricultural Cooperative Service (AGR), 6

AF   Air Force Department (DEF), 6, 7, 44

AG   Attorney General (JUS), 13, 19, 20, 30, 39, 44, 48, 49

AID   Agency for International Development (IDCA), 16, 22, 38

AMS   Agricultural Marketing Service (AGR), 6, 15, 20, 23, 24, 31, 32, 39, 47

ANT   Antitrust Division (JUS), 7

APHIS   Animal and Plant Health Inspection Service (AGR), 6, 9, 26, 28, 31, 38, 39

APO   Acquisition Policy Office (GSA), 24

ARMY   Army Department (DEF), 7, 44

ARS   Agricultural Research Service (AGR), 6, 13, 14, 25, 28, 37, 38

ASCS   Agricultural Stabilization and Conservation Service (AGR), 6, 15, 20, 24, 46, 47

ATF   Alcohol, Tobacco and Firearms Bureau (TRE), 5, 6, 7, 20, 21, 30, 40, 47

BE   Bilingual Education and Minority Language Affairs Office (EDU), 8

BGA   Block Grant Assistance Office (HUD), 16

CAB   Consular Affairs Bureau (STA), 11, 19, 22, 27, 28, 29

CAS   Civil Aviation Security Office (TRA), 25

CB   Census Bureau (COM), 11, 13, 17, 31, 38, 43, 45

CC   Comptroller of the Currency (TRE), 8, 13, 15, 21, 34

CCC   Commodity Credit Corporation (AGR), 6

CCCI   Command, Control, Communications and Intelligence Office (DEF), 17, 33

CDC   Centers for Disease Control (HHS), 5, 12, 19, 27, 39, 48

CEA   Council of Economic Advisers (EOP), 10, 17, 24, 46

CEP   Compensatory Education Programs Office (EDU), 12, 30, 31, 33

CEQ   Council on Environmental Quality (EOP), 5, 19

CG   Coast Guard (TRA), 9, 11, 17, 25, 28, 29, 32, 36, 37, 44, 45, 47, 50

CIA   Central Intelligence Agency (EOP), 19, 28, 31

CIC   Consumer Information Center (GSA), 13

CID   Civil Division (JUS), 8, 12, 13, 19, 20, 29, 30, 32, 40, 42, 50

CMS   Committee Management Secretariat (GSA), 5

154 Abbreviations/Index

VHSRA   Veterans Health Services and Research Administration
           (VA), 25, 26, 42, 48

VISTA   Volunteers in Service to America (ACTION), 49

VPO   Veterans Programs Office (EDU), 48

WB   Women's Bureau (LAB), 15

WCP   Workers Compensation Programs Office (LAB), 51

WHO   White House Office (EOP), 19, 21, 39

WIR   Wages and Industrial Relations Office (LAB), 49

YDB   Youth Development Bureau (HHS), 34

House Committees

AG   Agriculture, 6, 9, 11, 12, 13, 14, 15, 16, 17, 20, 21, 22, 23, 24, 25, 26, 28, 29, 30, 31, 32, 36, 37, 38, 39, 43, 45, 46, 47, 50, 68, 69, 70, 71, 94, 101, 121, 123, 124, 137

AGI Aging, 5, 68, 69, 70, 71, 95, 101, 121, 123, 138

AP   Appropriations, 9, 14, 16, 19, 23, 24, 27, 68, 69, 70, 71, 94, 95, 96, 97, 101, 121, 122, 123, 124, 127, 128, 129, 130, 131, 132, 133, 134, 135, 136, 137, 138

AR   Armed Services, 6, 7, 11, 17, 23, 24, 28, 31, 32, 33, 34, 35, 36, 44, 45, 46, 49, 50, 68, 69, 70, 71, 94, 96, 97, 101, 121, 123, 137, 138

BA   Banking, Finance, and Urban Affairs, 5, 8, 10, 12, 13, 14, 15, 16, 17, 20, 21, 22, 23, 24, 25, 26, 27, 28, 29, 30, 34, 35, 36, 39, 41, 44, 50, 68, 69, 70, 71, 94, 95, 96, 97, 102, 121, 123, 124, 137, 138

BU   Budget, 9, 10, 14, 17, 24, 40, 45, 46, 48, 69, 94, 103, 121, 123, 138

DC   District of Columbia, 16, 69, 71, 96, 103, 121, 124, 137

ED   Education and Labor, 5, 6, 7, 11, 12, 13, 15, 16, 17, 18, 20, 21, 23, 24, 25, 26, 30, 31, 33, 34, 36, 37, 38, 39, 40, 41, 42, 44, 45, 46, 48, 49, 50, 51, 68, 69, 70, 71, 94, 95, 96, 97, 103, 121, 124, 137, 138

EN   Energy and Commerce, 5, 6, 7, 8, 9, 10, 11, 12, 13, 14, 15, 16, 17, 18, 19, 20, 21, 22, 23, 24, 25, 26, 27, 28, 29, 30, 31, 32, 33, 34, 35, 36, 37, 38, 39, 40, 41, 42, 44, 45, 46, 47, 48, 49, 50, 68, 69, 70, 71, 94, 95, 97, 104, 121, 123, 124, 137, 138

FA   Foreign Affairs, 6, 7, 9, 11, 13, 15, 16, 17, 19, 20, 22, 26, 27, 28, 29, 33, 34, 35, 36, 38, 42, 45, 47, 48, 49, 68, 69, 70, 71, 94, 95, 96, 97, 106, 122, 123, 137

GO   Government Operations, 5, 7, 9, 10, 12, 13, 17, 18, 19, 20, 23, 24, 26, 27, 28, 30, 31, 37, 38, 39, 40, 43, 44, 45, 48, 50, 68, 69, 70, 94, 95, 96, 97, 107, 122, 124, 138

HA   House Administration, 7, 10, 13, 14, 18, 20, 24, 25, 26, 31, 32, 34, 38, 39, 48, 68, 69, 70, 94, 95, 96, 97, 108, 122, 124, 137, 138

IN   Interior and Insular Affairs, 9, 12, 15, 16, 17, 18, 19, 21, 22, 23, 24, 25, 27, 28, 29, 30, 31, 32, 33, 34, 35, 36, 37, 38, 41, 42, 43, 47, 49, 50, 68, 69, 70, 71, 94, 95, 96, 108, 122, 123, 124, 137

INT Intelligence, 28, 70, 71, 94, 108, 122, 124, 137

JU   Judiciary, 5, 6, 7, 8, 9, 10, 11, 12, 13, 14, 16, 17, 18, 19, 20, 21, 22, 23, 24, 25, 26, 27, 29, 30, 31, 34, 35, 36, 37, 38, 39, 40, 41, 42, 43, 44, 45, 46, 47, 48, 49, 50, 68, 69, 70, 94, 96, 97, 109, 122, 124, 137, 138

MM   Merchant Marine and Fisheries, 6, 12, 18, 19, 22, 25, 29, 32, 33, 36, 37, 44, 47, 48, 49, 50, 68, 69, 70, 71, 94, 95, 96, 110, 122, 123, 124, 137, 138

PO   Post Office and Civil Service, 11, 17, 20, 23, 24, 25, 26, 30, 31, 36, 37, 38, 39, 40, 42, 49, 68, 69, 95, 96, 97, 111, 122, 124, 138

PW   Public Works and Transportation, 6, 8, 9, 10, 15, 16, 18, 21, 22, 24, 25, 28, 29, 32, 34, 36, 38, 40, 41, 48, 49, 50, 68, 69, 71, 96, 97, 111, 122, 137, 138

Senate Committees

Joint Committees

Appropriations Subcommittees

AGR   Agriculture, Rural Development, and Related Agencies, 6, 9, 11, 12, 14, 15, 16, 17, 20, 21, 23, 24, 25, 26, 28, 29, 31, 32, 36, 37, 38, 39, 43, 45, 46, 47, 68, 69, 70, 71, 94, 95, 121, 124, 127, 137

COM   Departments of Commerce, Justice, State, and the Judiciary and Related Agencies, 5, 6, 7, 8, 9, 10, 11, 12, 13, 14, 15, 16, 17, 19, 20, 21, 22, 23, 24, 25, 26, 27, 28, 29, 30, 31, 32, 33, 34, 35, 36, 37, 38, 39, 40, 41, 42, 43, 44, 45, 46, 47, 48, 49, 50, 68, 69, 70, 71, 94, 95, 96, 97, 121, 122, 123, 124, 137

DC   District of Columbia, 16, 71, 121, 124, 130, 137

DEF   Defense Department, 7, 11, 19, 23, 24, 28, 31, 32, 33, 34, 35, 36, 44, 46, 49, 50, 69, 70, 71, 94, 121, 122, 130, 137

ENER   Energy and Water Development, 12, 15, 18, 19, 21, 27, 29, 35, 36, 37, 38, 40, 41, 42, 50, 68, 69, 70, 71, 94, 95, 96, 97, 121, 122, 123, 124, 130, 137

FA   Foreign Assisance and Related Programs, 7, 20, 22, 26, 29, 33, 38, 49, 68, 69, 70, 94, 95, 96, 97, 122, 124, 131, 137

INT   Interior Department and Related Agencies, 6, 7, 9, 12, 17, 18, 19, 21, 22, 23, 24, 25, 26, 27, 30, 31, 32, 33, 34, 35, 36, 37, 39, 40, 41, 42, 43, 45, 47, 50, 68, 69, 71, 94, 95, 96, 97, 121, 122, 123, 124, 131, 137

LAB   Departments of Labor, Health and Human Resources, and Education, and Related Agencies, 5, 6, 7, 8, 9, 10, 11, 12, 13, 15, 16, 17, 18, 19, 20, 23, 24, 25, 26, 27, 30, 31, 32, 33, 34, 35, 36, 37, 38, 39, 40, 41, 42, 44, 45, 46, 47, 48, 49, 50, 51, 68, 69, 70, 71, 94, 95, 96, 97, 121, 123, 124, 132, 138

LEG   Legislative Branch, 10, 13, 14, 18, 24, 27, 31, 32, 44, 49, 68, 69, 70, 94, 95, 96, 121, 122, 123, 124, 133, 138

MC   Military Construction, 33, 68, 71, 94, 121, 133, 138

TRA   Transportation Department and Related Agencies, 6, 8, 9, 10, 22, 24, 25, 28, 29, 32, 34, 36, 37, 38, 41, 43, 44, 45, 47, 48, 50, 68, 69, 70, 71, 95, 96, 97, 121, 122, 123, 133, 138

TRE   Treasury, Postal Service and General Government, 5, 6, 7, 8, 9, 10, 11, 12, 13, 14, 15, 17, 18, 19, 20, 21, 22, 23, 24, 25, 26, 27, 28, 30, 31, 34, 35, 36, 37, 38, 39, 40, 42, 43, 44, 45, 46, 47, 48, 49, 50, 68, 69, 70, 94, 95, 96, 97, 121, 122, 123, 124, 134, 138

VA   Departments of Veterans Affairs, Housing and Urban Development, and Independent Agencies, 5, 6, 7, 8, 10, 11, 12, 13, 14, 16, 18, 19, 21, 23, 25, 26, 27, 28, 30, 33, 34, 35, 36, 37, 38, 40, 41, 42, 44, 45, 46, 47, 48, 49, 50, 68, 69, 70, 71, 94, 95, 96, 97, 121, 122, 123, 124, 135, 138

About the Compiler

JERROLD ZWIRN is a reference librarian in a Washington, D.C. public library. He is the author of *Congressional Publications* and *Congressional Publications and Proceedings* and has contributed articles to *Government Publications Review*.

www.ingramcontent.com/pod-product-compliance
Lightning Source LLC
Chambersburg PA
CBHW050228270326
41914CB00003BA/623